In 1986 John Marsden spent three weeks at a friend's house in Torquay, writing the first draft of a novel for teenagers. The novel was rejected by six publishers before being accepted by a new Sydney firm, Walter McVitty Books. Published in 1987, under the title *So Much to Tell You*, it became one of Australia's great literary successes, winning a number of major awards, being translated into eight other languages, and achieving record sales.

Since then John has written five other novels for children and adolescents, all of which have been enthusiastically received by critics and by young readers. The most recent, *Letters from the Inside*, was a runaway hit.

John has also achieved success in other fields. His speeches and workshops on language, literature and writing have taken him to all parts of Australia and have enhanced his reputation as a teacher. He is in constant demand as a 'writer in residence' at schools and other institutions.

## Also by John Marsden

# JOHN
# MARSDEN

## Take My Word For It

*Lisa's Journal*

**MACMILLAN**
AUSTRALIA

First published 1992 by Pan Macmillan Publishers Australia
a division of Pan Macmillan Australia Pty Limited
63-71 Balfour Street, Chippendale, Sydney

National Library of Australia
cataloguing-in-publication data:

Marsden, John, 1950- .
    Take my word for it.

ISBN 0 7329 0765 9.

    I. Title.

A823.3

Typeset in 12/13 pt Andover by Midland Typesetters
Printed in Australia by The Book Printer

To Jeremy Madin,
one of my teachers.

## Acknowledgements

Thanks to the following for some of the stories in this book: Will Bowman, Adam Butterworth, Jenni Conner, Claire Coombe, Amy Curnow, Natalie Deans, Jonathan Geddes, Lucinda Gubbins, Sarah Morgan, Kate Mortimer, Angus Rigby, Josh Roydhouse, Nerissa Rutledge, Peta Sherwood, Sarah Tobias, Julia Utz, Tom Watson.

Special thanks to Emma Lee, Danielle Cooper and Jo Hayman for information and advice on rowing.

Special thanks to Mrs Margaret Hagger and Anthony White, Robert Paganin, Andrew Lampert, Kate Wignell and Catherine Pierce, for help in preparing the manuscript, and also to Jessica Russell.

And special thanks to Bec Joyce.

This seems an appropriate time to thank also people who, usually unwittingly, contributed stories to *So Much to Tell You*. They include Erle Cramer, Jenny de Goursât, Brian Morris, Jim Wild, Olivia Plumbridge, Tessa Harmer, Ann Poyser, Fiona Koch, Emma Crombie, Fleur Spriggs, Jodie Foreman, Kate McPhee, Ilka Rowe, Clive Moffat, Sir James Darling, Rebecca Joyce, and the late, much loved David Weeding. And of course John Mazur, Kay Nesbitt, whom I've never met, and the original 'Marina', whom I met briefly in Sydney around 1969.

Hi Journal, Mr Lindell, whoever's reading this. My name's Lisa. Not Sad Lisa, like in the song; more like the nursery rhyme:

> What's become of poor old Lisa
> Why's she sitting up a tree sir?
> Won't she wave to you or me sir?
> Can she see what we can't see sir?

I used to love that when I was little. There're not too many poems about Lisa, because it doesn't rhyme with much. Just 'mesa' in Geography, and I don't even know what that is. A kind of plateau, I think.

Is this what we're meant to do with these Journals, Mr Lindell? Rattle away like a train in a tunnel? Seems pretty slack, if you don't mind my saying so. Shouldn't we be doing subjects and predicates, like we did with Mr Aspen? Do you remember Tarryn Mortimer, who you taught last year? She used to say she hoped I'd get you for English, but I don't know if I'll like your style. At least it should be interesting—I just don't know if it'll help us pass exams.

Think I'd better do my Maths before I get in trouble tomorrow. Goodnight Journal, from me and Alex the Bear.

Dear Journal and Mr Lindell: Mr Lindell, I think it's a bit of a rip-off when you don't read these, because how will you see if we're improving, or using them properly? I didn't mean to be rude in class but I think it's all a bit pointless, and I usually say what I think (which is why teachers don't like me much).

Alex the Bear would like to say 'Hello' but he's not feeling well. He was chucked out of the dorm window last night by a certain person whose name I won't mention because I don't dob, but it starts with 'C' and ends with 'y' and has five letters. Anyway, this all happened after lights out, and I had to go down and rescue him without getting caught, which is not easy round here. And he was lying in MUD, which he does not like (why should he, poor little bear?). I think he thought it was Vegemite, which he does like so he was a bit confused.

Anyway he had to have a bath, and he's still upset.

I'll get Cathy back tomorrow—by the time I'm finished with her teddy he'll be stuffed in more ways than one.

Cathy's good value but generally this is not a great dorm. Everyone keeps asking us about the new girl, Marina. 'What's she really like?' How should we know? She doesn't seem to want to have anything to do with us, although I know it's not really us (Mrs Graham explained all that). But no-one comes near our dorm—we hardly get any visitors. They all go to Dorm D, where Kerry and Gabrielle are. I know it's not Marina's fault, but still.

I'm looking right at her now, because I've pulled my desk around a bit to get near the window. She's huddled over her books, like a hunchback. She doesn't seem to see or notice anything, and she never looks in anyone's eyes. She never even looks at their face. Her hair's quite long, dark, and she's got it tied back tonight. Usually it hangs long down either side of her face. The right side of her face is fine but the left half, the side I'm looking at, is a bit of a mess. It's all crinkly and wrinkly and red. You know how skin's meant to be soft—well, this part of her face looks hard and plasticy. In fact her face looks like a plastic plate that's been put on a hot stove. It's not easy to look at her.

## FEBRUARY 8

I did all my other Prep first tonight, so now I've got a bit of time to write in this. There's only one problem—I've got nothing to say. Nothing happened today. This was a day of nothing. A nothing day that was full of nothing, all day long. Nothing, nutting, nothing.

Friday night's the worst for Prep. No-one's in a mood to do any work, and they always put the strictest teachers and prefects on duty. Mrs Graham, for example, and Marisa Chan. Marisa's sweet, but you wouldn't want to be on her wrong side. Tracey didn't do her job this morning (she's on Dorm Vac). Marisa went and found her and told her to do it, but Trace just went to breakfast anyway. Melt down! Marisa met her coming out of the Dining Hall, and I swear, it made Krakatoa look like a fart in a bathtub. I've never seen Trace move so fast.

Marisa'll be a good House Captain I think. At least you know where you are with her, and she's not corrupt like last year's prefects. They all smoked and drank, but they busted other people for doing the same things. And they made us buy stuff for them at the tuckshop all the time, out of our own money. To tell you the truth, I'd love to be House

Captain, even though I know I haven't got much chance. I won't be campaigning for it—there's no point. I've made too many enemies.

We vote every year for prefects but I don't know how much notice Mrs Graham takes of it. She says she does, but I doubt it. Marisa would have won the students' vote, but I don't think Sally Becker should have been Vice Captain, and I'm sure hardly anyone would have voted for Skye Bayliss last year. I know I didn't.

## FEBRUARY 11

Hi Journal, how are you today? Hope you had a good weekend. I didn't open you once. But I admit I thought about you. A few times things happened and I thought, 'I might write about that in my Journal.' I can see how there's a danger of getting hooked on you.

I've never kept a Diary before. What's the difference between a Journal and a Diary, Mr Lindell? Must ask you in class.

I got in a few fights at the weekend. First weekend back—great start. I just don't like this dorm much. I was in a good one for the second half of last year, with my best friends, Issy Eastwood and Kizzy Tan. Issy, Kizzy and Lizzy, that's us. Now they're both in Dorm C and I'm on my own in B. The way they pick the dorms is really off. You write down two people you want to be with and two people you don't, but it's a bit like voting for prefects. I reckon Mrs Graham shoves the papers through the shredder. She seems to set out to break up every friendship she can. Term one last year she filled the dorm next to her flat with all the quiet, well-behaved kids. It was so obvious. We called it Square Dorm. This year there's one that's got nearly

4

all Asian kids, and Kate calls that Chinatown. Kate's one person I put that I didn't want to be with, but here she is, in the very next bed. I remember when she started at Warrington, halfway through last year. So funny. She came storming in with about six suitcases, dropped them all in a heap on the floor, kicked one of them across the room and said: 'Geez I hate this place.' From the look of the cases you'd have thought she was a real splendo, but she didn't talk like one. I knew her sister a bit— she was kind to me when I first arrived (she was a prefect)—but she was even louder than Kate, and her parties were legendary.

Anyway, Kate wasn't too bad to share with for two terms but I don't know how I'll put up with a second year.

I thought Sophie Smith would be a pain in the butt too, but she's been OK so far.

The one who really drives me to the North Pole is Ann Maltin. She makes me so mad! I want to pick her up and shake some life into her. Basically, she's a suck. 'Oh Mrs Graham, you haven't signed our Prep Diaries.' 'Mr Bostock, you forgot to set any Prep.' 'Miss Curzon, do you want me to do Marina's job for her?' I'm the one who does Marina's job nearly every morning, but Ann gets all the credit. I hate people like that.

That brings me to Marina. Now honestly Mr Lindell, do you think the school should take students like Marina? I mean, I've got nothing against her, but I reckon it's cruel sending her to boarding school. She should be in a hospital or something. And it's hard on us, not just because of jobs and stuff, but because she depresses everyone. People go quiet when she comes in. And the way she keeps to the walls. And her face—I couldn't look at her at first. I guess we'll get used to her eventually, but I hope she doesn't get worse, being with us.

5

I wouldn't be surprised. We're not a very good influence on anyone.

Do you think she used to be pretty, Mr Lindell? I think she might have been. The first time I saw her, her back was to me, and because she's got a good figure I was expecting her to be good-looking, you know how you do. But when she turned round I just gasped—I couldn't help it. I've felt mega-guilty about that ever since. I hope she didn't notice. Her face is so . . . I don't know . . . raw looking. And around her eyes—I suppose she's had plastic surgery—have you noticed those little ridges and lines? It makes my eyes water to look at them.

The thing is, she's got beautiful eyes, but you don't notice them till you force yourself to look at her properly. Now I love her eyes—they're so dark and deep and soft.

I reckon they should have done to her father what he did to her. They should have boiled him in it.


## February 12

I'm so depressed tonight. This place grinds me down sometimes. It's not really the school this time though; it's a story that Emma wrote, that she gave me to read. It's called 'Over The Edge' and it's about a kid who gets dumped on once too often by his parents and he ends up O.D'ing. It just had a bad effect on me, reading it.


## February 18

Yikes, you take a few nights off, and suddenly you've missed a week of this thing. It's definitely Mr Lindell's fault. If he checked them properly I'd do it properly. Oh well. I'll try to write a bit tonight, but I'm so stuffed after tennis all afternoon, then we had to do two chapters of Science and a Maths worksheet. Plus there's a French test tomorrow . . . irregular verbs. All of them seem irregular to me.

Chloe came down to see me yesterday. It was hard talking to her. She brought some tuck, which was good, and her new boyfriend, a guy called Hamish. I swear, she has a new boyfriend every week. Last Christmas she bought a card with 'To My Boyfriend' on the front, but she made sure she didn't fill in a name till the last minute. Anyway, I suppose I should be glad she came. At least she's trying. But why can't I talk properly to her? She asked me what subjects I was doing, what the teachers were like, what my dorm was like, if I needed any money, whether I'd heard from Mum or Dad. I asked her who'd done her hair, how her tennis was going, what work was like, whether she'd been to any good parties, how Ilka was. But we didn't really talk once.

Hamish is a bit of a spunk actually. I think she's done quite well for herself this time. He's tall, with curly hair, and a bit pale, but he dresses well and he did crack some good lines. He works for his parents, in a ski-hire business. I think he's a fair bit older than Chloe.

The tuck was good, but can you believe it, I put it in my locker, and by tonight three Mars Bars had gone and, I think, a can of drink too. This place is full of kleptos. It makes you sick. Emma said I should go and see Mrs Graham, but what's the good? I tried that last year and she didn't do a thing, just told me I should take more care of my stuff. So instead I made a speech at the start of Prep, and said I wanted it all put back, no questions asked, by lights out. I know it won't be though.

Dear Mr Journal, sorry I'm neglecting you a bit. You won't be getting much attention tonight either, I hate to tell you. It must be hard being a Journal—so closed and quiet for days on end, then coming to life for half an hour when someone opens you and puts a bit of breath into you.

It's only five minutes before the end of Prep. I've hardly got anything done tonight. The French test yesterday was such a disaster that we have to do it again tomorrow, but I don't think I'll go any better. Then I had a fight with Sophie—my first one, although I don't think she's ever liked me much. But she was being such a bitch to Marina. Marina, she annoys me too. I think people should show a bit of guts, instead of sneaking round the place like a shadow. I know she's had a hard time, and it's terrible what's happened to her, but she's not the only one, and she sure doesn't help herself.

I was watching her a bit today but you have to be careful. If she thinks you're watching she becomes self-conscious and hides, or makes like she's busy. Like in Maths, she was sitting next to Cathy, and everyone was looking at Cathy while she was answering some long problem, and Marina just kept her head down and pretended she was writing. But I could see what she was doing: drawing faces in her book. I've seen her do that quite a lot.

At mealtimes she always sits near big groups, but if they talk to her she moves away quickly. And I don't know if I'm imagining this, but I reckon she hangs around the phone a lot when people are talking to their parents. She always seems to be there, I don't know why. It just struck me tonight.

Speaking of phones . . . I wish Huw'd ring. I like him, but he is slack. I've rung him the last three times, and it's such a hassle. It's the same for people ringing here I guess. You wait ten minutes for someone to answer, then you wait ten minutes for them to find him, and half the time he's not there anyway, and that's cost you every coin you've got. Last week I think they forgot me completely—I hung on for half the night, then got cut off without any answer.

## FEBRUARY 21

This weekend's the first Exeat Day, the only way to get out of here short of tunnelling. Issy asked me to go out with her parents but I said Chloe and Hamish were coming down again. They're not, but I hate wrecking people's exeats all the time by going out with them. It's not fair to them. Issy hasn't seen her parents for over three weeks and she's entitled to the time. Then Tracey asked me too, and I used the same excuse. I think everyone's going out except me, but I don't, repeat, do not care.

I feel so disgusting tonight. I pigged out on a whole block of peppermint chocolate. Why do I do these things? I just took off the wrapper and tore open the foil, thinking I'd have one row, four squares, and then stop . . . ten minutes later I was licking up the last crumbs and feeling sick and revolting already. I'll have to go for another run tomorrow. I do all that training and then blow it in one big binge. My ambition is to win the biathalon. I came fifth last year, which wasn't bad for Year 8, and since then Holly, Liz Matthews and Liz Chen have left.

We had to write a poem for Prep. Yikes! I can't write poems. He gave us the first line and we had to do the rest. Mine was:

> *In the silence of the night* (he gave us that)
> *The house was dark and tense.*

9

*I looked at the sky and thought,*
*But nothing made any sense.*
*I looked at the moon and the clouds,*
*I saw the shape of a bird.*
*I said a silent prayer*
*And wondered if anyone heard.*

We've been passing them around all through Prep. People seemed to like mine. Sophie wrote:

*In the silence of the dark*
*I thought of Steve and thought of Mark.*
*I thought of David, Will and Rick,*
*Jeremy, Richard, James and Nick.*
*Alex, Trent, Serge and Ben*
*Where are you guys? I need some men!*

Way to write, Soph! She was pretty proud of that.

I liked Cathy's poem the most, but she's the best writer in the class.

*In the silence of the night*
*I walked across a plain*
*Of falling flowering snow*
*And gentle dancing rain.*

*I came to a rippling river*
*Near a smooth and ancient hill.*
*Where the snow was soft and even*
*And the wind and stars stood still.*

*And there I saw the colour*
*That I'd been looking for,*
*A little green by the river,*
*A tree that grew on its shore.*

Dear Ms Journal, I got heaps and heaps of work done tonight, while everyone else carried on like immature idiots. The latest craze is spitballs. They get gobs of paper, slag on them endlessly till they're soaking wet, then chuck them at each other—or at the walls when the tutor turns her back.

Kate used yellow paper for hers, that left nice yellow stains on everything.

In the middle of all this, Miss Curzon, who was on duty, caught Sophie with one in her hand, that she was getting ready to throw. 'Put that straight in the bin Sophie,' Miss Curzon said. Miss Curzon never shouts, but you know when she's serious, and she was serious. 'Oh Miss Curzon, I can't,' said Sophie. 'He's my pet.' She was cuddling it like it was a mouse or something. 'His name's Albert,' Sophie said, looking round at Kate to make sure she was laughing. I hate the way she does that. Miss Curzon started shouting then. I don't blame her. Sophie's always so rude to her.

I tell you what though, Ms Journal, if they start mucking round after Lights Out again tonight I'll be into them like a nuclear missile. Tomorrow's a big day for me—there's rowing all day, plus I want to go for a run and a swim before breakfast. Kate's so inconsiderate that she'd talk all night, even if you're sick or something.

I want to be totally stuffed by Sunday so I can just sleep all day, while everyone else goes out with their families.

Dear Journal, or Mr Lindell, whoever I'm writing to, I'm in the cruddiest mood, so don't expect any great words of wisdom. Had a massive bitch fight with Sophie last night, then one with Ann this afternoon. Wonder who'll be next? Line up folks, to be blown away by Cyclone Lisa. But honestly, I've asked Sophie about sixteen times not to smoke in the bathroom. I hate it. The fight with Ann wasn't so bad—I thought she'd dobbed on Issy to Mrs Graham (Issy got three hours for getting into the kitchen on Friday night and knocking off some Milo) but Ann swore she didn't, so I ended up believing her.

Then, on Saturday, while I was rowing my guts out, some klepto took ten bucks from my drawer. Honestly, I've never been in a dorm where so much stuff gets kleptoed. It's disgusting. Soph reckons it's Marina, and Trace reckon's it's Emma, but I don't think it's anyone from this dorm. Trace is playing detective—trying to work out who was in the dorm on their own on Saturday—but she's not getting far.

Just about everyone's had money taken, and other stuff too. It's really quite off. You don't know who to trust.

The only thing about Saturday was that I was wrecked by the end of it. I ran eight k's before breakfast, then we rowed till our arms were like dog food. Kizzy was crying from start to finish of the last sprints. Me, I love it. I want Eddie to drive us even harder. I wanted to go for a swim after training, and I would have too, if we hadn't had an extra Inspection at five o'clock (Kate's fault).

Went to Sick Bay yesterday, even though I hate going there, but I thought I had the flu. She just gave me Panadol. I chucked them away—I can't take tablets any more. I choke on them now.

Dear Mr Lindell, do you think bears get periods? Alex seems very moody today, and off his food. I guess male bears are exempt.

I ran twelve k's this afternoon—did the Horseshoe crossie, then kept going out, past the tip and back along the beach. Cathy came part of the way but she didn't do the extra bit.

Mr Lindell, you know what Tracey said to me after English today? She said: 'The reason you've got no friends is that you don't tell anyone your problems.' What a bitch! I hate the way they tell everyone every single detail about themselves. I don't like talking about myself. Is that so bad? I mean, what's talking going to do?

If you ask me, it's dangerous. Once you start, you don't stop. There's things I have to keep secret, and it's easiest to do that if you don't talk about yourself too much. It cuts down the risks.

Marina's got the right idea, I reckon. Anyway, my life's so seriously stuffed that there's nothing I can do about it. My Mum and Dad are never going to get back together, and I don't even want them to. There's no way Dad's ever going to buy 'Connewarre' again. That'd be the only thing that would make me happy. No, that's not true—it's too late for Dad just to buy it back, as though that would fix everything. My ambition is to get enough money when I'm older to buy it myself, and live there full-time.

Oh, I'm too depressed to write any more.

Wow, the fan sure got splattered tonight. Kate caught Marina with one hand in her locker and

Kate's Rock City shirt in the other. Kate went off like a space shuttle, grabbed Marina and chucked her half way across the dorm, yelling and screaming as only Kate can. As soon as Marina got a chance she snuck out of the dorm and disappeared, which turned out to be a major problem when we couldn't find her again. Eventually we had to tell Mrs Graham, and the prefects got sent out to search. They found her in the Bag Room having a nervous breakdown, so now she's in Sick Bay for the night, and we're all in trouble.

It beats me how Marina can steal stuff and yet we end up in trouble.

Still, as Mrs Graham said, we don't know for sure that she was stealing. The trouble with Marina is you never know where you are with her, 'cos she doesn't defend herself. But I don't think Mrs Graham was very fair to us. We've been pretty good to Marina, if you ask me. She hardly gets a hard time from anyone, and we often do her jobs for her, and we're always offering to help her or give her things. It's a bit hard when you don't get any response though.

I wonder if she was knocking off Kate's shirt. She wouldn't want to be. But she might have just been admiring it, or she could have found it lying around and been doing her a favour by putting it back. Kate's pretty sure it was in her locker though.

Anything's possible, but we'll probably never know the truth. Wonder if she took my ten bucks?

*FEBRUARY 28*

Rowing was so slack today. Eddie didn't turn up, so Mr Bostock looked after us, as well as the Thirds, and I mean fair enough he had to give the Thirds most of his time, but he could have given us a few minutes at least. Instead he sent us on a run for about half an hour then just had us do sprints up and down the river. Because he wasn't watching, no-one tried much. Ho hum, what a waste of time, what a useless afternoon.

## MARCH 5

Tracey's right about one thing. I don't have any close friends. I don't know if she's right about why, but the way I see it, a lot of people like me OK but that's where it stops. The funny thing is that I haven't got any serious enemies at the moment, except Ann maybe. Even though I have quite a few fights, I try hard to get on with everyone most of the time. I'm always sharing tuck and lending people stuff and helping with jobs, and I'm pretty good friends with people like Issy and Kizzy and Trace. But no-one was there when I really needed them. Oh I suppose I should learn to ask, but I don't seem too good at that.

Today, for instance, we had to clean the boats, and I ended up doing ours myself, 'cos all the others made excuses or hypo'd out of it. Then at tea I sat with Marina 'cos she was on her own again and looking pathetic. Then I spent most of first Prep teaching Sophie how to do sine and cos and tan. Sometimes it all gets a bit too much. Sometimes I feel like doing terrible things. That last time haunts me. I don't want to remember it, but it sneaks back into my mind.

## MARCH 6

Chloe rang tonight but I wasn't in much of a mood to talk. She stayed with Mum last weekend and they went to 'Her Majesty and Mr Brown', then to Mt Sandon on Sunday. Wish they'd taken me to 'Her Majesty'—I'd like to see that.

Last time Chloe rang I asked her to look for my old ballerina box when she went to Mt Sandon. It's nothing much—just a tacky old music box that has a dancing ballerina when you open the lid. But when I was a kid I thought it was the greatest thing I'd ever been given. I'd begged for one for a year, and finally got it for Christmas—I can't remember whether it was from Santa or who. I loved it so much. The trouble is, I was here at school when everything got packed and moved, and so much of my stuff got lost. Maybe it was just thrown out, I don't know.

Anyway, when I asked Chloe tonight, she said she hadn't had time to look for it. God she's a selfish bitch. It's pathetic of me to want it, I know, but I just do.

The ballerina's stupid when you think about it—the way she just goes round and round.

## March 7

Marisa Chan asked me today if I'd organise the Debating teams for Years 7, 8 and 9. I was really flattered. I like doing jobs like that. The first Year 9 team is going to be Cathy Preshill, Rikki Martin and me, then we'll probably change it for the next one. The topic is 'Winning is Everything' and we're the Government, which suits me, 'cos winning is everything for me.

It's against St Margaret's, on the 21st. They're always pretty good. We'll have to get a move on.

I ran the 8k course tonight. These creeps in a car were following me along the road section—three or four of them, real losers, making smart comments.

It's happened before, but I never know what to do about it. If I dob on them I won't be allowed to run again, not on my own anyway. I have to run to live. I breathe through my feet.

## March 12

Gee Mr Lindell, I've been a bit slack with my Journal these last few weeks. Sorry about that! When I look at Cathy's, and see pages and pages in it every night I feel pretty bad. I'll try harder, I promise.

There's been plenty of action tonight anyway. Mrs Graham's just been in here cracking a psycho about Trace and Emma who got back from Exeat severely off their faces. Trace chucked all over the bathroom floor. I ended up having to clean it up and put her to bed—she was giggling and falling over and wanting to talk to everyone non-stop. Then the moment she was in bed she suddenly dropped into a deep sleep and started snoring. What a mess. They're pretty dumb.

It was a shock for Mrs Graham though—Trace and Emma are real try-hards, normally.

## March 14

Mr Lindell, do you think it's fair that you can't ring your mother even if she's left a message asking you to ring? Two days ago Mum rang and left a message with whoever was on phone duty, for me to ring back, and I've been trying ever since, but there's always someone on the phone. Then tonight I was going to Prep and saw it was free and I rushed over and started dialling the number, and before I'd even finished dialling, Mrs Graham was out of her flat yelling at me. It's so unfair! And the more

17

I tried to explain, the more mad she got.

You know what I love about teachers? They ask you a question, like 'What are you doing on that phone?' and then when you say, 'Well, I was just ringing my . . .' they yell, 'Don't answer me back!'

It's hard to keep your sense of humour sometimes.

Wonder what it's about? Probably Easter. Chloe and I are going to Hawaii with Dad. Can't wait! They reckon it'll still be warm enough to swim. I'm so excited—I try not to think about it, so I don't get too churned up. He told Chloe he's booked us business class, for a bit of an extravagance. Hope he can afford it—I'm grateful but I wish he wouldn't waste money like that.

But what if Mum's sick or something? I'm so cut off here. I hate the way this place does that.


## MARCH 15

Dear Monsieur Diary, this debate's more trouble than it's worth. I've been trying to organise a meeting—shouldn't be hard with three people—plus Miss Curzon wants to be there, because she's our coach. But someone's always got something else on, and Rikki doesn't know if she can do it at all. We were going to have a meeting this afternoon but the rowing bus was so late that we didn't get back till tea had started. Cathy's collected some great quotes though, from a book in the library. 'Every time you win, you're reborn; when you lose, you die a little.' That's from a guy called George Allen. Then there's one from someone called O. J. Simpson: 'Show me a gracious loser and I'll show you a perennial loser.' I agree with that.

Ann's in Sick Bay at the moment, having a good bludge. She's so weak. Every time there's a crossie she gets a note from Matron to say she's got stomach cramps. She must have a period a week. An hour before she went to Sick Bay she was in the dorm listening to my 'Black as Sin' tape and eating Caramellos.

I finally got through to Mum. She only wanted to know whether I'd have time to go to the orthodontist at Easter, when I'm due for my next visit. I said I would. She told me 'Wombat' Edgar had died: he was one of our workers on 'Connewarre'. He would have been the oldest one but he wasn't that old. After we sold the place he worked for the new owners for a few months, then he went to 'Blendon' and worked for the Kirbys. Mum didn't know much about how he died: she just saw it in the paper. I'm pretty cut about it, to tell you the truth. 'Wombat' drank a lot but he was good to us kids and he was a good worker. When I was little I used to follow him round for hours, and he'd always bring the poddy lambs to me. He had a dog called Jess: I wonder what's happened to her.

I tried to ring Huw too, for someone sympathetic to talk to, but I got chucked off the phone by a Year 11 girl, Jayne Butler, who's probably the biggest bitch in the entire house.


MARCH 16

Got back early from rowing, so I did the Horseshoe crossie again. Everyone thinks I'm mad but I don't care. I want to get fit, and I want to lose weight.

I think about Hawaii as I run, and I imagine what it'll be like running along the beaches there. The trouble is, Dad's let us down so many times in the past that I know I'm stupid to pin too much hope on this trip. At first I didn't let myself think about it, but it's finally got through to me and now I dream about it all the time. But I swear, if he stands us up on this, I'll never forgive him: never, never, never.

Don't think I've ever written in my Journal at weekends, but I'm so bored and fed up I thought it'd be something to do. Can't wait till Easter and Hawaii and tropical nights and mangoes and pineapples, and big dark guys in colourful shorts coming out of the surf with the water running off them, and their white teeth shining. Most of all though I want to spend some time with Dad, and talk to him, really talk to him, the way some girls seem to talk to their fathers. I don't want to be selfish, but in a way I wish Chloe wasn't coming, so I could talk to him on my own. We've never really spent any time together, just the two of us, and when we have we've never talked about much.

I spilled my guts badly in the dorm Friday night, when Emma started saying how her parents had split up and now they won't have anything to do with each other and she has to pass messages from one to the other. Last year her mother was going to fly out here for Speech Day but then she found Emma's father was going to be there, so she wouldn't come. That started a whole big discussion about parents. After a while, for some reason, I joined in and told them how my parents split up the day I started school here, last year. They drove me here and dropped me off, acting like normal, then they went home and packed up and moved out. Mum went to Mt Sandon and Dad went to his flat in South Mandrill. He put 'Connewarre' on the market the next day. Then they wrote me letters to tell me what

20

they'd done. I didn't tell these guys the whole story: how I'd caused it and everything, but I told them enough. Too much really. I don't like it when people get all mushy and sympathetic. But they were OK.

Yesterday we had the WRC Regatta and I rowed like I wanted to lift the boat out of the water, but we only came fourth. It's so frustrating. Kizzy's good, and Rebecca's OK—at least she tries—but Kate is just too slack, and as for Myra! (she's our cox). I wish we had Tash back, but she got put up to the Thirds. Myra abuses us so much when we make a mistake and her steering's hopeless—she nearly put us into an MLC boat on the way down to the start.

Just for fun I went in the single sculls, and amazed myself by winning the U17's. There were only four starters, but still. I got quite a good time and won by about two lengths.

Today hasn't been much. There's a tree I sit in when I want to get away from everyone, and I often go there on Sundays. I read a book, or I watch all the happy families and wonder if I'll ever deserve to join them. Lately I've been sharing my tree—with Marina. She perches there like a terrified rabbit . . . not that I've ever seen a rabbit up a tree . . . and we both watch the free show up and down the drive. She's a sad case, Marina. After a while you don't notice her face any more—she's just another person around the place. But the trouble is after a while you don't notice her at all. She's like a ghost in the dorm. Then you think, 'Gee I've been ignoring her for ages', and you feel guilty and try to be friendly again.

I wonder if she'll ever talk. She must, surely. You can't exist without communicating.

Miss Curzon said she'll have some surgery on her face eventually, but she has to finish growing first.

I've gotta go—it's nearly tea-time. At least writing this has filled in an hour or so. I'm not looking forward to tea—Sunday tea's always the worst meal of the week. Oh, I nearly forgot! Sophie got busted for smoking this morning. Mrs Graham found her in the locker room with her cigarettes on the bench beside her, right out in the open. Fair up, I reckon. She only got three hours, which is pretty lucky. She has to do them before she goes home for Easter though.

Only four more nights' sleep, then I'm on the plane!

## MARCH 20

Dearest Journal, today I got great news, wonderful news. Miss Warren told me at lunchtime I was going up to the Thirds. I'm absolutely rapt. I'll be the highest placed rower in Year 9. It's a great crew: I'll have Tash as cox again, and Skye Wills, from Year 11, is stroke—she's really nice. Then there's 'Stevie' Szanto, who's also in Year 11, and Annabel Kimpton from Year 10. I think I'm replacing Brenna Buckley, which I'm a bit embarrassed about. I'm sorry to be leaving my crew too—well, most of them, especially Kizzy—and I don't know what I think of having Mr Bostock as coach. But I'll make it work. It's such an honour. It's a big change for them, with the State titles on April 29—just over a month away.

I can't write any more—we've got a debating meeting in a minute.

Three nights to go! Hawaii—I love you.

The debate's just finished, and we didn't get Prep set tonight, so I might as well write in this for a while. It's a bit stupid—we have to sit here for twenty minutes, till the bell goes, even though we don't have any work. We should have spun the debate out for the whole of Prep, but that might have been hard, seeing none of us spoke for our full time. We weren't very good, and we lost by about 20 points. Dr Whiteley was there, and she didn't look too impressed. I still think winning is everything, but we should have proved it by beating St Margaret's.

It was pretty nerve-racking speaking to all those people. Next time I'll have my notes better organised. I left out about three major points and stuffed up the ending.

I think it's because of Dad that I'm so keen on winning. He went to the Olympics and to two Commonwealth Games for his swimming—he was a middle-distance freestyler. He won two bronzes at the Commonwealth Games—one for 400 metres and one for a relay. My biggest ambition is to row in an Olympic crew. I've been waiting till Thursday to tell Dad about my going up to the Thirds: he'll be rapt.

Just two more nights!

MARCH 22

Got a message from Chloe that Hawaii's cancelled. Dad's too busy. I've got to go to Mt Sandon instead. It's typical. Trust him not to tell me himself. He wrecks me when he does things like this. I hate him, that's all there is to it. He's such a rotten, miserable, selfish slimebag. I thought we were really going this time. Congratulations Dad, Mr

Reliable—you sucked me in again. But that's the last time.

I hate the way I'm crying all over this page and messing up the paper. I'm going to stop writing.

## APRIL 3

I haven't done my Journal for two weeks, almost. Haven't been in the mood, plus we've had the Easter break. I've been rowing my skin off (literally—I've got beautiful blisters) and running. I'm trying to be nicer to people too—I think I was pretty bitchy for the first month or two of term.

## APRIL 4

Cracked an hour from Dr Thorley for nothing today—we're doing the feudal system in History, and she was saying how the moats presented problems for the attackers in their armour, and I muttered to Sophie 'Yeah, like rust,' and I got an hour for that.

## APRIL 5

Mrs Marina herself has just paid us a visit. I was so hyperactive with curiosity that I didn't politely go out of the dorm, like I should have, but instead stayed on my bed, pretending to read. First Marina came in, walking quickly on her toes and not looking at me. Then Mrs Graham, with this lady who I knew straight away had to be Marina's mum. She was tall, with red hair, and dressed in a black leather coat and tight black pants. Stunning stuff. Not a lot like her daughter. She had that bright lipstick on but she looked a bit tired—I think she's been overseas, so maybe she just got back.

What was funny was the way they managed to have a conversation without Marina ever saying anything. It was like: 'Do you need your winter dressing-gown do you think?' and they both looked at Marina, then Mrs Graham said: 'Well, the nights certainly have been crisp lately,' then Marina's mother said: 'What do the other girls have?' and they both looked at Marina again. But while they were looking at her, Mrs Graham was answering: 'Well, most of them do bring back a winter gown, even though the dorm is heated.'

Marina's mum asked Marina: 'Are all your new things marked? The things Grandma got you?' and Mrs Graham said: 'Matron takes care of all that. She's very thorough. She has to be of course!' and they both laughed politely and Marina's mum said: 'Yes, I don't know how you do it. So many girls!'

It went on like that for about ten minutes. I suppose it was a bit sad really. Mrs Marina just talked to her daughter like she was a girl in a shop.

Anyway, they went off to see Matron, while I kept reading 'I am the Cheese'. But about an hour later I had to go to the gym, and on the way I passed Mrs M sitting in her car. Mrs Graham had gone, and Marina had gone, and her mother was there alone, bent over the steering wheel. You could tell she was crying.

## April 6

I met this guy at the beach over Easter, when I went for a run late one afternoon. It was the only good thing that happened at Easter. His name's Peter Fallon-White, and he goes to Walford College. Saw him a few times after that and we talked a bit. He

seems a nice guy. Anyway, he rang up tonight—
it was quite good. I haven't heard from Huw in so
long I guess that's faded into non-existence. But if
he wanted to drop me I wish he'd done it face to
face, instead of not getting in touch, and having his
mates say he wasn't there whenever I rang up.

I haven't seen Dad for so long and I honestly
don't give a piece of popcorn and I really mean that.

Marina's freaking out now. Maybe it was her
mother's visit. She was pretty upset after the movie
Saturday night. I tried to give her a hug tonight
but she ran away.

## April 7

Friday nights are so boring. The latest craze is
to set the video to tape 'Those Around Us' during
the day, then replay it at night. Tonight they watched
two episodes in a row. Two hours of it, it's unbeliev-
able. Instead of doing that I talked to Cathy for ages—
there's no doubt about her, she's good to talk to.
She's in love with a guy called Andy who she met
at a party a few weeks ago. He sounds like a bit
of a winner. The photo she had of him wasn't too
flattering, but it was hard to tell—he was just one
in a big group, and they were all off their faces.

I envy Cathy her life. They live on a property
called 'Moonibah'. It sounds great, a lot like 'Connewarre' except that 'Connewarre' was on the coast.
I guess that's a big difference, but the lifestyle sounds
so similar . . . I don't know why I liked 'Connewarre'
so much . . . the space, for one thing, and the stock-
work of course. Mum and Dad were better when
they were there too—not so many arguments. We
didn't have people coming and going all the time,
like at Mt Sandon. I get sick of all the visitors there.
'Connewarre' was peaceful. There were times when

I didn't have the least idea of what day it was. I remember so much of it—but not enough. I'm scared that if I don't remember every detail, then bits of it will die, piece by piece, paddock by paddock. I work hard at remembering it. I think I liked it most at night, when so many stars filled the sky I could see my way to the cabin by their light. I liked the possums too, the way they used the network of trees like a giant expressway system. I especially liked the dry summer nights when the harvesting went late, with the headlights and spotlights shining so strongly, and the machinery throbbing away. For a while we had some Boobook Owls in the garden. They lived in the tops of the trees during the day and flew around at nights. One night as I went to the cabin, one of them was on the washing line, less than two metres away, watching me with great interest, but without moving or showing any fear. It was all wonderful to me: I believed in everything while we were there. I even liked things other people didn't, like the clatter of the grasshoppers in the dry grass, and the smell of sheep and the smell of fertiliser and the way little black ants had huge conventions in the kitchen when we left any food out. The dogs were great. We had lots of dogs, always at least four, sometimes six or seven. They were so good with the sheep. They'd ride on the back of the motorbikes, or in the ute, but they loved their work like no human I've ever seen. We had one old dog, Mollie, she was so clever. We used to tie a pup to her sometimes, when she was working sheep, so the pup would learn from her. She resented it though—I think she thought it was undignified. One time she disappeared for a few minutes and when she came back to the yards the pup was gone. We all went searching, but it took about ten minutes to find him—somehow she'd managed to dump him in the water tank, and he'd been paddling for all that time to stay afloat. He was tired when we found him—I don't think he'd have lasted much longer.

It was a hard life for the dogs in a lot of ways. They were kept in a row of cages, with a kennel and a concrete run in each one, and were chucked a few handfuls of meat and bones each night. They got so excited when you went near them.

Often I'd come home from the paddocks about sunset and, coming along the ridgeline opposite the house, I'd see the windmill and the old church with the red sky behind them. It'd be still and quiet, and I'd stop and look and feel how peaceful it all was. It made me realise how impossible it'd be to be a painter, because you'd never capture that light.

We always had trouble getting a good manager but the last one was good. He'd just finished doing all the fences when I came away to Warrington, and of course I never saw it again. But I heard that the new owner sacked the manager and tried to do it himself, and that now it's all run down and covered with weeds and stuff. Dad told me once I should marry the new bloke and then dump him, and that way I could get the place back. I don't think that's much of an idea.

Tomorrow's my first race with the Thirds. I'm so nervous my heart's racing already. If the boat goes as fast as my heart we should be OK. I don't want to let them down, that's the main thing. I'll never sleep tonight.

Marina's a bit of a mess again, and is back in Sick Bay. Just when you think she's getting somewhere she goes into another tail spin. I went over to visit this afternoon but it's hard—there's a limit to how long you can stand there talking at her. I took her some tuck—she never seems to have any. Actually she doesn't seem to have anything much— clothes included. She looked really sad today, huddled up in bed, sucking her thumb, wearing those off old brown PJ's that look like they came from the Salvation Army. I'm going to suggest to Cathy we put a bit of work in on her hair when she gets back to the dorm. She's got nice hair, and I reckon it'd look pretty good cut shorter, with a bit of colour, and brushed more often.

I'm meant to be organising another debate, but we'll have an all new team I think. Maybe Issy'd be good, and Sarah Venville—she's good at everything.

Had a letter from Peter Fallon-White today. He doesn't write all that well, but a letter's a letter, so I'm not complaining.

Oh, I forgot to mention the rowing! So much time seems to have passed since Saturday. Anyway it was great. It's so different in the Thirds! They get on so well together, and the standard's much higher. It's good having Tash coxing again too— she's so positive and cheerful, and she's always cracking sick jokes when we need a bit of a lift. Mr Bostock's better than I thought he would be. He tells us to row with our heads, not our muscles. We were in two races on Saturday and won them both, even with Annabel catching a crab about 300 metres from the line. Mr Bostock teaches us to time each stroke so that we catch the boat at peak momentum—'getting the run on the boat'. Rowing's the best thing in my life right now.

Mr Ross is on duty tonight. Nice guy, but he's kind of gullible. People do pretty much what they like when he's on. For example, you say you have to test each other for French or something and he lets you go up to the dorm or in the Common Room for most of Prep. When he catches you in the wrong dorm after lights out you just put your arm around someone and say they're upset and you have to talk to them.

Last week he caught Sophie having a smoke in the Drying Room and Sophie told him her grandmother had cancer and she was so upset she'd had to have a cigarette.

We're having a Talent Quest tonight, just Year 9s, and everyone has to go in costume and do something. Cathy, Trace, Sophie and I are going as strippers and singing 'In a Bar in Alaska'. Should be a bit of a cack. Rikki Martin's staying in our dorm, 'cos her parents are away—she's sleeping in Marina's bed. (Marina's still in Sick Bay). Rikki and Emma are singing this version of 'Jailhouse Rock' in Japanese. I can't wait to hear it.

I had another letter from Peter today. He's getting serious. He sent a photo—I stuck it over my desk. He wants one of me. There's one Kate took a while ago, when we were waiting for the bus to go downtown, that's not as ugly as most of them—I might send him that.

Went to see Marina again this afternoon after Rowing. There was a thunderstorm about 3.30 and it was too dangerous to go on the water, so we worked out in the Gym and ran a crossie. That meant we finished early.

This Saturday's the Riverside Gold Cup Regatta, then the CMC Invitation, then the State titles on the 29th. It's getting close. I'm nervous already. It must be bad being in the Firsts—imagine what they'd be going through. They're undefeated this season, which would make it harder in a way.

I think I can hold my place in the Thirds. Dad said he'd be coming Saturday. I don't care if he does or not. He thinks I'm still in the Fourths. I never bothered to tell him I'd gone up.

Marina looked OK, a bit better even. She'd hardly eaten any of the tuck I left her—just an Aero Bar. It's depressing seeing her like that.

It's hard to concentrate at the moment—Kate and Soph are having the most ginormous bitch fight. It's over this party in the holidays that Soph's going to—some guys from St Patrick's are having it. Soph said she'd get Kate an invitation but she hasn't done anything about it, and Kate thinks that's deliberate. It's more likely to be Soph being slack, but Kate's raging like a buffalo on heat. Here's how they talk— if I can get it down fast enough:

Kate: *Well you're the one who suggested it in the first place.*
S: *Oh! Good one Kate, really good.*
K: *Well you did.*
S: *Yeah, after you'd given me 20 minutes of how ripped off you were.*
K: *I just thought it wouldn't hurt you to do something for someone else for a change.*
S: *WHAT? Kate, you scab food, money, clothes off me all year long and then you say that? Whose top are you wearing by the way Kate?*
K: *Face it Soph, you're a tight-ass.*
S: *Ohhh! I can't believe you! Ask anyone! Lisa, am I a tight-ass?*
Me: *No Soph.*

S: *Cathy? Am I a tight-ass?*

Cathy: *Well . . .*

S: *Shut up Cathy. I know you hate my guts anyway. Ann, tell them. And remember who lent you white shorts for PE this morning.*

Ann: *You are pretty generous Soph. You've got a lot of faults but you're not a tight-ass.*

S: *Thanks a lot.*

K: *Soph you're turning this into a big joke. It's nobody else's business anyway. I wouldn't go to the party now if you paid me. All I'm saying is, you shouldn't make promises if you can't keep them.*

And so it goes on. Just a typical scene from Dorm B folks!


## APRIL 13

Dad rang again tonight, said he'll have me for the last week of the holidays. I can tell he's still feeling guilty about Hawaii. Not half as bad as I feel though.

Prep's ended and nearly everyone's rushed off to catch today's episode of 'Those Around Us'. Cathy and I are the only ones left here. Marina's still in Sick Bay—I took her over a couple of tapes tonight.

We've hardly any Prep all week, then tonight we suddenly got heaps. A page and a half of Maths, a whole chapter of Science, three 'mini essays' in History, and a chapter of 'Lord of the Flies' for English. I'll read 'Lord of the Flies' in bed, which is where I'm now going.

Mr Journal, the funny thing about chocolate is that the less I eat it myself, the more I like to see other people eat it. I'm always telling them to stuff more into their gobs. I give away practically all my own supplies. I have a chocolate calendar on my desk and a chocolate poster above my bed. But I haven't had any myself for about three weeks.

I've been sitting here reading Cathy's Journal tonight. She said I could. God it's different from mine. She writes so beautifully, and she decorates it and stuff like that. She writes about so many things— not just school, but home and about her family and how she misses them, and about things like ozone and Greenpeace and dolphins. I think those things are important too but I don't seem to write about them. This place sort of fills up your mind: being here 24 hours a day you don't seem to notice much that's happening in the outside world.

The number one leisure time activity here is gossip.

Cathy writes how she feels about things, too. It's honest. She wrote quite a lot about me. She said I'm a sort of a leader—people expect me to take charge of things, and they listen when I give an opinion. That all surprised me, but it pleased me too. She also said I'm too reserved—that I never tell anyone what I'm really feeling, and I make it hard for people to get to know me. I suppose that's like what Tracey said a while back. It's true. It's hard though. That's the way our family is. I'd never know how Chloe felt about the divorce, or 'Connewarre', or even getting dumped over the week in Hawaii. I'm a bit scared to say how I feel about all those things. I mean, I can say I feel bad about losing 'Connewarre', but that doesn't say anything. There was that night in the Dorm—that's the only time

I opened up at all, and that was partly to show Trace that I could. I don't know whether that was a good thing to have done, or not. I suppose it was. Well, I know it was. Cathy wrote about that in her Journal. I was moved by what she said. She does care about people. I don't know if I do. I think I'm really hard. I don't know if there's anyone I love. It's frightening to say that. I know I should love my parents and my sister and my friends, but I don't think I do. After I'd been here two months last year we had the Easter break, and I went to my father's flat at South Mandrill. After I'd been there a couple of days I did something terrible, something so awful I've never been able to tell anyone. I can't, even now. The funny thing was that no-one even noticed—that was the one thing I hadn't bargained on. Life's a tricky business. It's like Sophie and her bad habit of short-sheeting beds. Every night when you check the bed, expecting that she's short-sheeted it, she hasn't, and the one night you forget and jump in, she has.

Since those first few months of last year I've changed a lot, I think. My life seems to be in a slow spin. I don't think I'm going to be the kind of adult I dreamed of being when I was a kid. I envy the way Cathy writes. If I could say what I wanted to, about losing 'Connewarre', if I could bring it out of myself in words, this paper would be buried under the weight of it. For quite a while I wouldn't believe it had been sold—when Chloe tried to talk about it, I changed the subject, and when people at school asked where I lived, I told them it was 'Conne'. I still kid myself I live there sometimes. I tried to talk Dad into buying it back—I offered dumb things, like giving up my pocket money, or leaving school and getting a job. See, he says he can't afford it. But I think the fees here would pay for a couple of paddocks at least. I can't see why he didn't try to share farm it, or lease it, or even sell some and keep the rest.

At least I can write about 'Conne'. The other things I can't write about at all. It's late and I'll have to go to bed in a minute. I don't particularly want to, and I don't know if I'll sleep much, but I've got to try, with the Regatta tomorrow. God I hope we win.

## April 16

Dearest Diary, this is what happened. The weather was beautiful, the water was smooth, the wind was down. We drew lane one, which everyone said was the fastest. With everything going so perfectly I knew I'd catch a crab and fall out of the boat in the first hundred metres. We got an OK start, not as good as University, but not too bad. They had a length on us at the 600 and I was getting worried, but we were long and strong, rating 28, and c, c and c (cool, calm and collected). It was so different from the Fourths, where by this stage Rebecca would be screaming at Kate, I'd be screaming at Rebecca, and Myra would be screaming at all of us. But this time we did ten hard through the bridge and came out the other side just in front, then fought them all the way to the finish. It was great. We had so much power, rating 32 and storming home like seals on steroids. Warrington first, University second, Girls Grammar third and the water foamed around us like champagne.

## April 17

Tonight I thought I'd do something different and write about someone else. So this is my attempt to describe Sophie. Firstly, I've got to say that Sophie is incredibly funny. She's also wild, uncontrollable, unpredictable, noisy and impossible to live with. She's pretty—she's cut her hair short at the moment and she looks fantastic—and I love her voice. It's so husky, like a boy's when it's breaking. She doesn't like me very much—she thinks I'm bossy—but I can hack that. It's because she likes everything how she wants it anyway. She loves to be the centre of attention. She could be so smart if she worked, but she doesn't strain her brain—she's always telling Cathy she hates the way Cathy 'analyses' everything. Soph's got the concentration span of a Barbie doll.

Her best friend and worst enemy is Kate.

What I like about Sophie is that even in the middle of the biggest fight or the worst depression she always stops to laugh at herself, at the way she's going on. She always says 'Oh well' when she realises she's not acting very logically. For instance, she'll be ripping into Kate for getting us yet another extra Inspection because Kate wasn't ready on time, and Soph'll be burning up about it, and she'll say: 'And this is the second time this week we've had a 6.30 Inspection! And who got us the last one? Oh, it was me wasn't it? Oh well.' But that doesn't stop her—then she'll say, in a voice like a teacher. 'Anyway Kate, I just think you should have more considera-tion for other people', and we all crack up, but I honestly don't know if she's serious or not when she puts on that voice.

I think under it all Soph has no confidence. You can never pay her a compliment—she won't let you. She hates her parents. She mucks around at every-thing—it's as though she doesn't want to have a proper go at it, in case she fails. Or in case she succeeds. She takes the biggest risks—she could have been expelled about six times already this year.

She and Kate went into town at midnight at the start of last week—they caught a taxi at the roundabout and didn't come back till about three in the morning.

Another good thing about Soph is that she really is generous. She'd give you anything. You can't say you like anything she's wearing, or she'll try to give it to you. She'd give you the shirt off her back and the bra off her front. I think her parents must have heaps of money—she's got the best clothes of anyone in the dorm—but she takes the worst care of her stuff. She loses and breaks more things than anyone I've ever seen. She's also the cheekiest student to teachers that I've ever seen. When Mr Bostock was giving back tests the other day Sophie didn't hear him call her name, so he picked up hers and brought it down the room towards her saying, 'What do you want, Sophie, Room Service?' She just said, 'That's what you're paid for isn't it?'

He acted like he didn't hear, but I can't see how he could have missed it. Everyone in the room heard.

So, that's Soph, about the most unboring person I've ever met. I don't know whether I'll put down to be with her next year, but I know one thing, I wouldn't have missed it.


### April 18

I got a message to go see Dr Whiteley today, which had me a bit worried, but it was only for an Anzac Day service next week—there're two kids from each year, and she wants Rikki and me to go for Year Nine. It's quite an honour really.

We did this beautiful poem in English yesterday, called 'The Good-Morrow'. It's a love poem, written four hundred years ago.

*For love, all love of other sights controls,*
*And makes one little room, an everywhere.*
*Let sea-discoverers to new worlds have gone,*
*Let Maps to other worlds on worlds have shown,*
*Let us possess one world, each hath one, and is one . . .*

It's so sweet. I'm going to write it out in full and stick it on my desk—next to Peter's photo, I think. It's kind of ironic that the day after we did the poem, Cathy got a phone call from Andy to say she was dropped. So that didn't last long. She was so upset—I didn't realise she liked him that much.

We've got so much Prep I shouldn't be writing in this at all. It's hard to settle down to proper work though—my desk is next to the door into the dorm, and Ann's in there playing her violin, like she does every night. I know she has to practise, but she always spins it out twice as long as she should, so she can get out of Prep. And it's so boring. She plays the same tunes over and over, especially that theme from 'Second Coming'. She sounds like galvanised iron when you're pulling one sheet of it across another.

## April 19

Chloe came to see me again today. It is good that she does it. No guy in tow either, although she says she's still with Hamish. She said Dad's getting with someone, too. I really cracked at her, until she said, 'It's not my fault. Don't take it out on me.' We started talking a bit then. I asked her if she was glad they were divorced, and she said she thought it was better in some ways. She said she couldn't understand why it happened though—she thought they'd stopped fighting quite a few months before. I realised then that she didn't know the full story at all. That's good in one way—that she doesn't know I caused it. See, she was away a lot towards the end of that year—she'd been getting quite a lot of work catering and cooking and she was saving to go overseas. She didn't realise that the reason they'd stopped fighting is that they'd pretty much stopped talking. Actually that only struck me afterwards, and I was living at home full-time. Boy, was I ever dumb.

I asked her if she missed 'Connewarre' and she said she did. But . . . well, I know that's the truth, that she misses it, but I don't think she misses it the way I do. For me, it wasn't just land, it was the ground under my feet. The only thing I can compare it to is this: when I was about eight, Chloe, and whichever boy she was with at the time, took me to the Show. Now, they've got this thing there that I suppose everyone would have known about except me. It's called the Gravitron or something— it's a barrel that spins, and the floor drops away, and you're stuck to the wall by centrifugal force. But I didn't know any of that. Chloe and this boy told me they had a big surprise for me, and they made me shut my eyes while they took me in there and got me to stand against the wall, making sure I didn't get any clues about what was going to happen. Well, the thing started up, slowly at first, then faster and faster. That was OK, then suddenly I felt that I was a few centimetres off the floor. I couldn't understand how that could happen, as I hadn't realised that I'd moved, and I looked down so that I could get myself back on the floor. Then I saw that the floor had dropped away, and I had this absolute panic that the thing had malfunctioned and it was all falling apart—that it would fly to pieces around me. It took a few moments to realise that it was doing what it was meant to do. When I saw Chloe laughing, I started to understand. Then it just became a matter of surviving the ride, all the time wishing for death.

I didn't show a thing on my face though. I'm proud of that—not one flicker of fear. I wouldn't give them that satisfaction. At the end, when Chloe asked me what I'd thought of it, I just said that it was OK. I hope she was disappointed.

So, that's the best I can do to describe how I feel about losing my beautiful 'Connewarre'—the ground under my feet.

I'm pleased Chloe and I talked a bit though. This might sound big-headed but I think she does resent me a bit. She didn't do well at schoolwork or sport, then she got expelled from here in Year 11, so when I get good marks in tests, and get promoted in rowing, I imagine her thinking, 'I don't want to be outdone by my little sister.'

The thing I resent about her though, is the way she takes advantage of Mum and Dad living apart. She sees it as a good chance to get everything she can. The way she spends Dad's money is sickening. But I'd never dare say it to her face. I'm just little Lisa.

## April 20

Ran so many laps today. I'd normally do a crossie but there's been the odd car-load of drop-kicks around again and Dr Whiteley has banned crossies unless you're in a group of three and tell a teacher you're going. I like to run alone.

I hope we do well on Saturday, at the CMC. We're up against University again, and Muirfield, who beat the Thirds by half a canvas a few weeks ago.

And this time the Fourths are in the same race, which'll be interesting.

## April 21

Mr L, supposing you did something bad, something really bad, do you think your grandparents would see it from Heaven and be upset and angry at you for doing it? I used to worry about that a lot, but then one day I thought that if they were in Heaven they'd be happy all the time (otherwise it wouldn't be Heaven). So that must mean they wouldn't know about it.

Maybe a screen drops into place whenever you do something bad, so they can't see? But then they'd wonder what you were doing that was so awful. Oh, it's so complicated.

## April 22

Well, that was a scorcher. We got a stinking start—we were side-on when the starter gave the word. I think Tash was rattled by one of the officials yelling at us as we came up the river for the start—he thought we were going to get in the way of a crew that was racing down the course. Tash had it under control, but he didn't know that. So anyway, the gun went and by the time we got going we were very last. That was good in one way, 'cos University and MLC nearly crashed ahead of us. After a hundred metres the Fourths had the lead, or at least it looked that way from where I sat. Then came Muirfield, then University and MLC abusing each other as they tried to steer a decent course, then the legendary Warrington Thirds. Mr Bostock must have been wetting himself. We were starting to panic, Tash was yelling, 'Keep your heads up girls, get it together,' but we weren't making much progress. The others all caught the Fourths easily, but we still weren't functioning. Then Muirfield suddenly ploughed to a halt—we found out later their gate broke—and so we passed them, and even though that wasn't a great achievement it helped us settle down somehow, and we set out after the Fourths. I know it's wrong but I wanted to beat them more than anyone else in the race, and beat them by a good margin, too. I thought it'd be my fault if we didn't. And I know how badly they wanted to beat us.

Coming round the bend we hit the headwind, but Tash found us some dead water and we went for twenty hard. I was trying too much I think and I couldn't go with the flow, not using my head, not catching the run of the boat. Tash said, 'Hey Lisa, get with it.' We reached the Fourths; they were sweating and gnashing their teeth and both of us were catching MLC. But gradually we started getting away from the Fourths: out of the corner of my eye I could see Kizzy slipping backwards. 'Keep the pressure on,' Tash said. In the other boat I could hear Myra yelling, 'Shut up, shut up', and I gave a little grin inside. That was typical Fourths, fighting when things went wrong. 'Two hundred metres,' Tash said. 'come on Thirds, last effort.' I was level with the MLC bow but University looked out of reach. We settled down to grunt it out with MLC. Tash was red in the face, gripping the side of the boat and urging us on. I heard the bell as University crossed the line. But we had to beat MLC. 'Come on, come on,' Tash screamed. We were flying, together at last, their green singlets and red faces were so bright—I remember that more than anything—but the line was too close. A metre past the line we were ahead of them, but that was no use.

I was so disappointed. I thought I'd let them down. That was our last race against University and now they'd think they were better than us. And we'd wanted to test ourselves properly against

42

Muirfield. We still think we can beat MLC, but then we'd thought that yesterday too. All in all it was a hopeless effort. I think I'll take up free-fall bungy jumping.

## April 24

I'm going to write more about the weekend, seeing nothing much happened today. The Regatta was such a mess—hope we've used up all our bad luck before the big one on Saturday. Mr Bostock was calm about it but Miss Warren gave us a big lecture about our starts and our steering (Tash was not impressed).

The Fourths came last, not counting Muirfield.

Saturday night I was absolutely stuffed. I skipped the movie and went upstairs to the Year 11 cubes and talked to Skye and Stevie for an hour or so. That's one good thing about being in the Thirds— I get to talk to the Seniors much more. But I was in bed by nine o'clock.

Sunday Chapel was even more boring than usual. Halfway through the Responses Dr Whiteley stopped and made us start them again, because she said we weren't saying them in time. I think that's weird. Surely if we're praying it's up to us what speed we do it at. They're having a big crackdown on Chapel at the moment—even Ann got a det yesterday.

Then after Chapel Mrs Graham had this heavy session with us in the dorm. See, Marina was out on a double exeat, despite the fact that it was a closed weekend—but she was with a teacher (Mr Lindell), plus she never goes anywhere, so I guess it was fair enough. Anyway, Mrs Graham had a meeting with us about her. I was pretty surprised by what she said. She said we hadn't been very kind to Marina, that we'd left her out of things, that she'd promised Marina's mother that we were such a friendly group but that we'd let her (Mrs Graham) down. She asked us if we still blamed Marina for the kleptoing, and she said it would be unfair if we did.

There was a long silence and everyone seemed to be looking at me, so I spoke up. I was quite heated actually—must have been all the sleep I'd had the night before. I said I thought we'd been pretty good to her. We're always asking her things and trying to include her. We lend her stuff and give her stuff and crack jokes with her and we don't pay her out like we do to each other. In fact we stick up for her all the time. If anyone from another dorm says anything about her face or that, we practically shred them. I said we don't hold the kleptoing against her, 'cos for one thing it was never proved, but it's true that there's been hardly anything stolen since Marina got busted with Kate's shirt.

Marisa Chan was at this meeting, and she was OK. She said she noticed Marina wasn't slinking about the place like a hunted fox any more—she walks more confidently and has her head up more. But she still said we didn't treat her as a full member of the dorm.

Kate said it was pretty hard because she never gives you any encouragement when you do try to include her. Soph, in her usual outrageous way, asked how come Marina got special privileges, seeing she was meant to be treated the same as everyone else. Mrs Graham asked, 'What special privileges?' and Soph pulled the trigger and said, 'Well where is she right now? It's a closed weekend and she's on a double exeat,' which left Mrs Graham without much she could say, just making horrible faces.

I admit there've been some awful things done to Marina during the year: Sophie using her like a puppet is one that springs to mind. Trace renaming her Teddy 'Marina' when the teddy lost his grunt is another. But by and large I reckon we've been good to her—and good for her. I swear, there have been times when I'm sure she's smiling inside at the things that have happened. The other night, for example, Sophie was getting changed, and as she was struggling into her jeans (she's not getting any thinner, Soph) she moaned, 'Oh, I need to take a Panadol just to get my jeans on.' I happened to be looking right at Marina, and something definitely flickered across her face. I suspect it was that elusive smile.

## APRIL 25

Rikki and I went to the Anzac Service in town. It was OK, not as boring as I thought it would be, and it did get us out of an Astronomy test in Science. A few weeks ago we had that film, 'For Valour', and that changed my attitudes a bit. One of the guys in the film, who was killed in the evacuation from the beach, looked so like Peter. I was looking at the old diggers at the Cenotaph and trying to imagine them as the young guys in the film, but it was hard. They seemed so serious and responsible. In the film they were casual and carefree, not giving a stuff about anything. They were different from us, I think. In those days I don't think people our age questioned anything or analysed what was happening. Seems like the Government said, 'OK, there's a war, you blokes grab a uniform and get over there.' And they said, 'Oh yeah, righto, we'll have a bash at that.' Nowadays we'd say, 'Well, what's the war for? Who's fighting and why? What other ways out of it did you try before you declared war? Why don't you go yourselves if you're that keen on it?'

I admire those guys who went though, and I

felt really sad for them having so many mates killed or wounded, and I know we wouldn't be living in the kind of country we're in now if they hadn't gone.

## April 26

All I can think of is the Schoolgirls' titles on Saturday . . . I'm in a bad way, I tell you. I'm sleeping about as much as Alex the Bear, who has no eyelids, so his eyes are open 24 hours a day. Issy says Tash has been coxing in her sleep for the last week.

Kate talked me into putting some red in my hair tonight. But I think we overdid it—it looks pretty bright. Miss Curzon chucked a fit when she saw it but that's nothing to the one Mum'll chuck. She's coming to the Regatta, so she'll see it soon enough.

Mrs Graham's on a roll too. At tea she went sick at Sophie for taking salad when she already had a hot meal. Then at Assembly she realised a Year 8 kid had run away, and she went into a frenzy again. What I thought was funny was that she seemed more emotional about Soph ripping off some potato salad than she was about the kid who ran away. I mean, who pays for the food anyway?

## April 27

OK girls and boys, it's Auntie Lisa's laugh-a-minute time. Why do white sheep eat more grass than black sheep? Because there's more of them. What's stupid and yellow? Thick custard. What do you call an Eskimo's house if it doesn't have a toilet? An ig. Yes folks, and there's thousands more where they came from.

Mr Lindell, if you're never going to read these Journals, I guess we can write anything we want, whether it makes sense or not. Sally sells seashells by the quick brown fox. Hey diddle diddle, the cat and the crumpet, the cow jumped over a roundabout. The little dog laughed, and laughed and laughed, until its tongue fell out.

My favourite word is lambent. I'm not even sure what it means but it's beautiful, so I'll write it a few more times: lambent lambent lambent lambent lambent lambent lambent I think it's starting to lose its beauty lambent lambent lambent.

You know I seriously do like Peter. He wants me to go to a party with him on the first Saturday of the holidays. I rang Mum to see if I could talk her into it, but I hit a fresh complication—now Dad wants me to go to his flat for the first week instead of the last. He hasn't even told me, and Mum said it was stuffing up all her arrangements, so she wasn't in the best of moods. I tried to ring Dad but there was no answer.

I feel sick when I go near Dad's flat. Too many bad memories. I did something very stupid there, and I just don't want to think about it.


<u>April 28</u>

Fourteen hours from now we'll be lining up and Tash'll be reaching for the toggle and we'll be shaking so much that bits'll start falling off the boat. The forecast is for intermittent showers, clearing around lunchtime. That could mean anything.

One of my ambitions is to make the Firsts, and realistically I could. I could even get there next year, which I'd love to do, and which would be quite something, doing it in Year 10, but I don't know. If I'm this nervous now, what would I be like in the Firsts? And I didn't do very well last week.

I hope Dad turns up, so I can get him and Mum

47

together and work out the holidays. It's such a mess. Mrs Graham's been hassling me for travel arrangements, so in the end I told her I was getting the city bus and being met at Goold Street. That'll have to do.

Sometimes I'd love to have a really good friend, someone I could talk to about anything, and trust with a secret. I hardly seem to see Kizzy and Issy these days—we're only in the same classes for PE and French. But I was still reserved with them last year. There are things I want to talk about but can't. It gives me a big lump inside . . . maybe this is what being pregnant is like. I'll give birth to dark spidery secrets.

Rikki started calling me Refrigerator for a while last year, because she said I was so cold. I was even cold about that—I coldly asked her to stop, and she did. Inside I was crying.

Dad cancelling the Hawaii trip—that was the first time I'd cried for five years. I wasn't crying because I wanted to go to a tropical island and get a tan; I was crying because I wanted to have some time with Dad, and he'd let us down again. The last time I cried before that was when I was 9 and there was a barbeque at 'Connewarre' and one of the kids broke a necklace that Dad had given me. She'd borrowed it, and she'd worn it even into the dam, and someone grabbed her and the necklace broke and nearly all of it was lost. Anyway, Chloe found me crying and told me I was a baby, so I decided I wouldn't cry any more. I didn't either.

Gee, I was determined not to get serious in this Journal tonight, and look at me. This is not the way to prepare for the biggest regatta of my life.

Well, that's the end of the rowing season. I'm so sad, even if I hated it sometimes. But Saturday, oh Saturday, I'll never forget you. It was quite a race. MLC, Muirfield, PLC, Girls Grammar, St Margaret's and us. And after practising starts all week, we messed it up again—except that this time we got a second chance because St Margaret's broke and the starter recalled us. Skye turned round and said, 'Right girls, luck's running for us now, let's take it.' And the second start was good.

All the crews got off well though, and after a hundred metres we were still pretty much level. Then PLC started to drop out and Muirfield nudged ahead. We passed a group of kids from school who were on the bank screaming for us, and gradually we moved up to second. It felt better than last week—we were smooth, and catching the run of the boat. Muirfield hit some rough water and we gained a bit more. But to my surprise I saw St Margaret's coming through on the other side of the course and looking really strong: no-one had expected that. I thought, 'the bend'll sort us out' and it was good. Tash took the perfect line and we made up another length and caught Muirfield, but St Margaret's were still there. 'Come on come on come on,' I was saying to myself. Tash was saying, 'Keep the pressure on girls. Get it together two seat. It's the last race, put it in.' Muirfield wouldn't give up, and I thought St Meg's were getting a bit ahead of us. Going under the bridge they led us by a length, and we were equal with Muirfield. There was one gross moment as I realised we were being showered with spit by boys on the bridge, then Tash called for ten hard and away we went. The idea was to surprise the other crews, to jump them while we were out of sight. 'Use your heads girls,' Tash urged.

'Pressure in the stretches. More leg drive.' The boat seemed fast and eager this week. We came into sunshine again and looked across. We were an inch in front of St Margaret's, Muirfield were nowhere to be seen, but MLC had suddenly come up from nowhere. They'd pulled the same stunt we had. 'We can do it Thirds.' Skye's singlet, in front of me, was the wettest I'd ever seen it. I was aching, sweating, trying to find more energy from somewhere. I knew Tash was going to ask us for the big effort and I wondered if I could give it and prayed that she wouldn't ask for it yet. But sure enough, it was, 'Go for it girls, long and strong remember, this is what we've trained for.' And somehow, from somewhere some energy came. 'Pain for gain girls.' MLC were beside us and St Margaret's across the course. Muirfield were coming again. The MLC number two, I'd never met her but I knew her so well. The pain in their faces, must have been like ours. The boat so smooth but where was the finish line? God let it be soon. Tash was full on: 'Hard, damn hard. Hard back with those arms. Wind it up. Nearly there, fifty metres, crank it up. Go! Go! Go!' MLC slipping back slightly, and Muirfield half a length behind I was sure they couldn't catch us now, but St Margaret's, why hadn't anyone warned us about them? 'HUGE effort girls, HUGE,' Tash begged us. We gave it. The bell took me by surprise! I looked across the river and couldn't tell, then I looked at Tash's face, and I could tell straight away. WOW! You mean it? You're sure? Oh! We've done it!

Yes, I want to record officially here that Tash, Skye, Stevie, Annabel and I are the Champion Schoolgirl Thirds for this year. It was fantastic, just fantastic. And the Firsts won too—good on them. That means they stayed undefeated for the season. They get to go to the Nationals in two weeks, so there go their holidays. I just wish they had

Nationals for Thirds crews. We could have beaten anyone yesterday. I'm so happy about it, especially as it proves that my getting put up didn't do any harm to the crew. The Seconds came second and the Fourths came fourth, so really we should have come third.

MAY 1

Tomorrow's the last day of Term 1, thank God. I didn't think it'd ever finish. We haven't got much Prep and we're allowed upstairs to pack soon, which is always a good slack. There was meant to be a Debate against St Paul's tonight but they cancelled.

Dr Thornley grabbed me this afternoon and told me she wants me to be Captain of the Year 9A Basketball team next term, which is fine, except that we've got a match the first Saturday back! With no training or anything! It's going to be a massive embarrassment but we're in a town comp and they don't take a lot of notice of our term dates. Dr Thornley's arranged for us to have a first round bye, and a second round postponement, because we'll be on holidays. So our first match will be the other team's third—not a good situation. Everything just seems a huge anti-climax after Saturday. How can I think about Basketball? I can still feel that boat, so light on the water.

MAY 4

I'm glad I brought my Journal with me. I thought it'd be something to do. I knew I'd be bored, but not this bored. If things keep up I'll be watching 'Those Around Us'. I went for a run yesterday, and even further today, right up to Bowman's Hill, then

51

came back, rang Kizzy, rang Chloe, and started getting tea ready. I wanted to make a really good meal for Dad—I was going to do it last night, but he took me out to Mango's Restaurant, to celebrate end of term and the rowing. He brought along his 'friend', Lynette, who was OK. She was trying hard, got to give her credit. She's good-looking enough, but I don't think she's too smart. She's a lot younger than him. Actually she looked about Chloe's age. She works as a PR consultant for Troy and Foreshaw: pretty glamorous job.

I hope this meal works out. I kept sampling everything while I was doing it, and it seems OK. I've made avocado and zucchini soup, then chicken wings in honey to follow, then chocolate and rum mousse. I'm full already from all the testing.


## MAY 5

It's a year today since I thought I was going to solve all my problems right here in this bedroom. It seems so unreal now. I've managed to go a whole year without properly thinking about it once.

I remember the date because it was the fifth of the fifth, which was the day Gramps died, four years ago.

The great meal didn't quite work out last night. Dad rang about 8.30 to say he'd be late. That's sort of a tautology isn't it, to ring at 8.30 to say you'll be late for dinner? We did tautologies in English.

I chucked the food away.

I got really depressed after that. Maybe that's the reason I remembered this date.

## May 6

Only three days before I go to Mum's. I'm glad. I can't stand being alone in this flat. I keep meeting my own bad dreams.

Ran to Bowman's Hill again today, and then over to the Observatory and back through Meridian. I ran hard, to get away, then had a spa and felt better. We're going to see 'Out to Lunch' tonight, with Wendy and the Davisons and maybe the Peakes. Should be good, but I'd rather have been going to the party with Peter. I bet he'll go, and crack onto someone else.

## May 7

We've been at the football all afternoon. Norths won by four points—way to score guys. It's the first time I've seen them win in three years—I was starting to think I was jinxing them. Dad knew the full back, Andy Kobol, so we had a drink with him after the game. He's a nice guy. He said this season's their best chance for years, but I suppose they always have to think that, to be positive.

On the way back Dad started talking about the Olympics and everything. He doesn't normally say much about that. It was interesting. His father drowned when he was little—that's why he was so fond of Gramps, Mum's father. And his mother, who must have been a strong lady, made him take swimming lessons so he'd be safer in the water. But now Dad says he half regrets his swimming career. He says it gave him a lot of opportunities but, on the other hand, he didn't do as well in his schoolwork as he could have. He got enough marks for Uni but he didn't go—they were short of money—but the main reason was the swimming. He said the thing

53

he regretted most was that he didn't do anything with his mind for those years that he was swimming competitively. He said that his brain and his imagination went into stalemate for a long time, and when he did start using them again it was quite hard and he felt he'd fallen behind. 'Must have had water on the brain,' he said. He always turns everything into a joke. I wish he wouldn't sometimes.

Lynette came over about seven o'clock. Dad was down the street getting a video, so suddenly there I was alone with Lynette. And suddenly I was being a complete bitch. I don't even know why. I was sort of hating myself for doing it at the same time that I was doing it. I think it was because Lynette was trying too hard, if that makes any sense. She was trying to get me to talk about school and rowing, and in the middle of it I just turned on the TV and sat there watching it, giving little grunts and yes and no answers. I was so rude I embarrassed myself, but I didn't let her see that, and of course she was getting embarrassed and trying not to show it. Then I heard Dad's car in the drive and I jumped up and raced out there, pretending I was really keen to see which videos he'd brought.

## MAY 8

Ran early this morning, and made Dad come too. He's getting a bit pudgy. We just jogged round Lipman Park a few times. Then I went into work with him, like I used to when I was little. Mainly I went because I can't stand being on my own in the flat, but I had quite a good day in there. It's changed a lot. Dad's in a new office—a much better one, the one Mr Dunlop had before he retired. It's got a view over the Botanical Gardens—so beautiful. He's got computer screens in there now too, because the Exchange has gone computerised. There's a lot of new staff—Miss McDonald left and he's got a new secretary, who looks like Lynette actually. Trust Dad. I asked if she was Lynette's sister and he got quite annoyed. I also saw Oliver Boyd, who used to go with Chloe, and now he's working for Dad.

I just did odd jobs for Dad and for Mr Susanto. I filed a lot of stuff, mainly annual reports. And I went through all the job applications they'd had in the last few months, making sure there were no references or certificates that needed to be returned before the failed applications got shredded. Then I got lunches for a lot of people (I changed Dad's order from a pie to a salad roll, and he ate it). In the afternoon I helped with the photocopying and shredding, then went out and did some shopping. We got back here about 6.30.

## MAY 9

I'm so angry! Dad gave me a big talk about being nice to Lynette—I'm sure she dobbed on me. What does he want me to do, pretend I like her when I don't? I hate the way she practises her public relations on me. She came over last night again and asked me if I wanted to go to the beach today. I made a pathetic excuse about meeting Kizzy but it must have been obvious I was lying, 'cos I didn't try very hard to hide it. I had somewhere else to go, anyway.

Dad talks to Lynette like she's about ten years old.

I can't wait to go to Mum's.

## MAY 11

I got to Mt Sandon yesterday. It's been OK. Aunt Sophie's here, and Edward and Will, but not Nick—he's at a tennis camp somewhere.

We played tennis today. American doubles, and I got thrashed. The boys have improved so much.

Chloe's coming to tea tonight.


## MAY 14

Oh what a weekend. Mum had a dinner party last night that went till three in the morning. The Vincents stayed the night; they've just gone. Mum's energy never falters though. She was up at six and went for a run along the beach. There was a doctor at the dinner party, Dr Weatherly, and I think Mum's got her eye on him.

If you want to know the truth I hate the way they're linking up with all these new people—Mum and Dad I mean. We were all together once, weren't we? Now they're forming new groups, even new families maybe. I don't want that. I want to be back at 'Connewarre' with the friends we used to have. Is that so much to ask? Why are they doing all this?


## MAY 15

I don't know what's wrong with me lately. There are some entries in this Journal that I can't bring myself to read back over, they're so stupid. Yesterday's, for one.

Today wasn't bad. Went down the beach with Edward and Will. They're so funny—they tell all these radical stories about school. Makes Warrington sound a bit square. But I'm sure it's easier to get away with stuff at their school. We're watched twenty-four hours a day.

Mum and Aunt Sophie came down later. Aunt Sophie was paying Mum out about this Dr Weatherly guy. I didn't think it was that funny, but you never know how serious adults are.

Peter's coming over Wednesday. At least that'll help make up for my missing the party. I can't wait to see him.

## MAY 16

Had a good fight with Mum today, over nothing much. She wanted me to go shopping with them, I didn't want to go. She said if I stayed home I had to do the ironing, I said OK, but somehow didn't get around to it . . . could have been because I was on the phone to Peter half the afternoon. Mum got home, went sick, and I said some fairly off things, I must admit. But I was still going to do the ironing— I wasn't trying to get out of it. Better go and apologise—something I am not experienced at, am not good at, and definitely do not like doing.

## MAY 17

Peter, Pierre, Petras, Pedro . . . no, not Pedro. There's so many ways of writing it. I looked up a dictionary of names at the newsagent tonight when I was getting the paper. They said Peter was out of fashion for a while but made a comeback when 'Peter Pan' was published. Somehow I don't think my Peter would have much in common with Peter Pan. Wasn't Peter Pan the boy who never grew up? Peter Fallon-White's grown up, that's one thing I can vouch for.

We had a breezy time. He came to lunch and did a good suction job on Mum, then we walked down to the beach and sat there and talked—and a few other things. Then we went to the shops, then he had to go. I miss him. I missed him from the moment he got on the bus. I've rung him tonight already—can't wait till tomorrow when we can talk again—he's ringing me.

## MAY 20

It's nearly the end of the holidays and my secret mission has failed so far. I wasn't going to write about it in here but I've changed my mind. I want this to be a true record of the year, so when I'm an old grandmother (Mrs Fallon-White?) I can read it and see what I was really like, what I was thinking about and feeling.

Four times these holidays (today was the fourth) I've taken a no. 8 bus (no. 18 from Dad's flat) to Mercer, and sat in the milk bar diagonally opposite 61 Dobson Road, and taken as long as mortally possible to eat a sandwich and drink a coffee, while I watched, hoping to see them. I saw Mrs Aston once, going in, but no sign of Miranda. I'd recognise her if I saw her.

It's frustrating that I don't know the truth about Mrs Aston and Dad. I just want to know. I think I'd know if I saw Miranda.

Now I'll have to make sure I hide this Journal extra well for the rest of the holidays. Mum'd be so upset if she found I'd been there, looking for them.

## May 21

Went to Peter's tonight for dinner. His father drove me back here a few minutes ago. I had a great time! It's a funny old house but really sweet. And his parents were funny—they had about six arguments while I was there, but no-one seemed too worried.

Peter's father used to be in the Navy. He's older than the fathers of most kids my age but he's a cool guy. He calls everyone 'darling'—his wife, Peter, me, the dog, the cat. He looks like a Norwegian sailing captain—fluffy white hair and red cheeks. He dresses like an out-of-work gardener—one of the arguments was about his not getting changed for dinner.

Mrs Fallon-White's tall, but with this great face, great bone structure as my mum would say. I'd love to photograph her, or paint her. She's very calm—Peter says she meditates and does Yoga and stuff. She's got a notice in the kitchen above the phone, that says, 'The greatest risk is to take no risk.' I like that! That's my philosophy! I'll have to remember it next term when Mrs Graham stands there draped in jewellery, telling us we can't wear earrings, and a little voice inside me is saying, 'Put your hand up and ask her why.'

## May 22

We all go back to school tomorrow but Edward and Will went home today to get their stuff. For some stupid reason we ended up playing Monopoly all morning before they left. It was so dumb, one of those games that go on forever. By the time we gave up Will had about twenty million dollars, and Edward was about twenty million in debt, and I was even. Will's so annoying when he's winning though—I nearly rammed his hotels, cards and money down his mouth a few times. But we had some laughs.

## MAY 25

I am so stressed out. This Basketball is the biggest mess I've ever seen. It's so different from rowing, where it was all super-organised. We're meant to have a team for Saturday; we've had two practices, one of which was a joke, and at the end of today's practice Dr Thorley told me to pick a team and put it on the board by 9 am tomorrow. I don't think she realises it's not quite that easy. Ann's not back from holidays, Kate reckons she's going on exeat, and Sarah says she's got Osgood-Schlatter's. I said, 'Well you've got to have a note from Matron,' and Sarah went off at me, saying, 'You're not a teacher.' OK, I know that, but if the teacher won't act like a teacher, what are you supposed to do?

We're going to get thrashed anyway, I know that, but it'd help if people made a bit of an effort.

There's so much happening already. We've got another debate in a couple of weeks, there's a huge History assignment on the Crusades that we're getting tomorrow, and there're auditions for the School Play soon, too—I wouldn't mind having a go at that.

Meanwhile Marina sits there like an island, while we storm around her. I wonder how much of all these details she takes in? She probably sees more than we think. She writes in her Journal quite a lot, probably about us. God knows what she thinks of us. It's a madhouse tonight.

This Crusades assignment is enormous. I don't see how we're going to get it done. Title page, three maps, time line, half a dozen essays, three biographies, illustrations, bibliography, index. Mr Journal, I don't like your chances this term.

Went and had a good talk to Skye Wills tonight. We hardly ever seem to penetrate the holy land of the Year 11 cubicles, but sometimes I'd rather talk to them than the Year 9's. Skye especially. She said they went to Spectacle Beach for most of the holidays and half the school was there. That's what I hate about this place. Unless you dress a certain way and talk a certain way and go to certain places for the holidays you're out of it. Skye said she saw the Firsts on TV—they came third in the Nationals. I was annoyed with myself for forgetting to watch, but TV doesn't play much part in my life, so I never think to look at the programme guide.

Skye knows the Fallon-Whites so we had a good goss about them. She really likes them. I can relate to that. She said Mrs Fallon-White had cancer years ago, but she came through it, but that's why they didn't have any more children—she couldn't. I was shocked—Peter never told me that.

Nothing else is very interesting. Cathy's got a man, a guy called Guy. Marina's birthday is soon, according to Miss Curzon, so we're going to get presents for her and give her an extra good day. She seems OK after the holidays—I don't know where she went. I wonder how different this dorm would have been without her in it. Honestly, when she was coming here, I didn't know what we were getting. I remembered the court case from the papers—it wasn't that long ago—but you never think people will step out of the news into your own life. I thought she'd be, I don't know, more psycho, screaming and having nightmares and chucking fits. She's the opposite of that though. She goes on with her life in quite an organised way now—she gets herself ready in the mornings and is on time for everything. But she doesn't look at us—she looks at what she's doing, or into the distance, thinking her own thoughts. You try to say hello but she won't meet your eye. I'm beginning to think she's very strong actually, even if she is frustrating to deal with. She's stronger than me in some ways. I gave up, she hasn't.

Cathy reckons she's going to invite her home for mid-term. Good on her—I hope she does. Cathy's family's really nice—they took me out for lunch one day last year.

Well, there's not much to do. I can't start the Crusades assignment till I can get to the library for some books. I could do the Title Page I suppose. Mr Ross is on duty—I might ask him for some paper. Hope we get a good supper tonight—it's Matron's night off, and the Relieving Matron does great suppers. Better ones anyway. Everything's relative, as Mr Ross keeps saying. The game tomorrow (basketball) is at 9.30. We've got a massive squad of six, so too bad if someone's injured in the first two minutes, or gets fouled off.

I'm exhausted. It's tiring being back at school. Think I'll catch up on some Z's.


MAY 28

Everyone's on leave except me, as usual. Even Marina's gone, to the Lindells again. You don't normally get so many people out on the first weekend. Issy's around somewhere but I haven't seen her.

I sat in my tree for hours this afternoon, reading a book.

*What's become of poor old Lisa,*
*Why's she sitting up a tree sir?*
*Won't she wave to you or me sir?*
*Can she see what we can't see sir?*

Can I see anything? I don't think so. I don't understand a lot of things. It's being able to see the inside of things that matters—anyone can see the outside, and it doesn't signify much. Take life at 'Connewarre', for instance. I only ever looked at the outside life there. I looked at the paddocks, the trees, the sky, at the blackberries growing in the old boundary rider's hut, the Boobook owls perched above the willie wagtail's nest, the burnt out car among the trees and rocks on a hilltop on the far side of the property. The thing is, though, that the heart of a property is the house, and I never looked, I wouldn't look, at what was going on in that house. I was outdoors from dawn to dusk. Inside the house it was cold and uncomfortable, although I was only dimly aware of that—I didn't think about it. I only came in for meals and sleep.

It was the same with the magazine picture that wrecked everything. Mrs Aston and Miranda. I showed it to Mum quite innocently, didn't I? 'Look Mum, how come Mrs Aston doesn't come here any more. She used to come so often. I didn't know she had a daughter. She looks like that baby photo of Chloe, doesn't she? I thought it was Chloe at first.' Was it all innocent? That's what I'm not sure of. Even though I didn't know or understand, I had some deep, strange, vague feeling that I was stirring up trouble, doing something dark and wicked and wrong. It was the same as a year or so before that, when I'd let Mum catch me eating some chocolate I knew Chloe had shoplifted, and when Mum said, 'Where'd you get that?' I'd innocently said, 'Chloe gave it to me,' knowing Chloe would get into a lot of trouble.

63

With the magazine it was vaguer than that—a vaguer feeling of mischief—but I knew, or at least thought it possible, that I was nudging open an evil door. I had a feeling something was lurking in there.

Well, if I wanted to cause trouble, I sure succeeded. I lay in bed that night listening to what I'd caused. My eyes were open and I practised keeping my face even and strong and cold. I was determined not to be a baby. But I felt sick at what I'd done.

I feel sick writing about it, remembering it.

After that I started thinking that my family would have been better off if I'd never been born.

Oh, by the way, we actually won the basketball. Can you believe it? I can't. If ever a bunch of losers went onto a court with no hope at all, it was us. But we battled away, scored a few baskets now and then, and got ourselves out of it whenever we seemed to be heading into a catastrophe. We did it on guts, not class or skill. We won 28–24. I'm still amazed.

## May 29

It's getting good and cold. I don't mind the cold weather, especially when it means snow. I hope it's a good season. It opens officially next weekend but there hasn't been a flake so far. Still, 'late snow is good snow,' Mr Susanto always tells us. At least we can count on Dad to take us skiing—he loves it so much that he'd go even if he had to ski barefoot. Um, come to think of it, that mightn't work too well.

Mr Lindell, Rikki told me today that she hands in her Journal every few weeks and you write comments in it. She said you do it for anyone who asks. Now that's very sly of you—I didn't know we could do that. The big question is, do I want to do

64

it? There's a lot of stuff in here that I wouldn't like to have anyone read. On the other hand . . .

I'll have to think about it.

We had a proper basketball practice today. What a relief. Just lay-ups and dribbling practice, but boy did we need it. Afterwards Trace and I took a quick illegal and shot up to Bridgland's for a milkshake and a general pig-out. Putting down incriminating evidence like that is one reason why I shouldn't hand this Journal in. Self-dobbing. Mr Lindell, how do we know you don't photocopy the ones you read and hand them over to Mrs Graham or Dr Whiteley? I mean I know you wouldn't, but still.

Tracey's a funny kid I reckon. A lot of people have got the wrong idea about her—they go on their first impressions and don't look any closer. Actually my first impressions of her weren't too good. I thought she was a bit of a slob. She is big, but it's more that she's big-boned, if you know what I mean. At the same time she can be lazy—physically lazy anyway—but she does a fair bit of Prep. The first few days I was here Trace seemed like one of those background people who agree with everybody. Then I noticed that everything she said had a cutting edge to it—she was always hacking a chunk out of me with these little spiteful comments. Then we got put on a PE assignment together—we had to prepare and teach a skills lesson to Year 6—it took ages, because we were a bit hostile to each other, but in the end it worked out really well. We got the giggles when we were demonstrating our lesson to our own class, and we just collapsed after it, and I think that's when we became friends.

Trace is one of those people who pass through the school without the teachers noticing. She never talks to them. But she's got a network of kids who know her and who she hangs around with and I think she has a big influence with them, although it's not that obvious. She isn't liked much in dorm B, or she wasn't at the start of the year, but she's getting more popular now. That's because people know her better. Actually the teachers are noticing her more too—she's getting in more trouble. Plus she's got a man now—Stewart Pace his name is, he goes to Grammar—and I think that's making a bit of a difference to the old Trace. If she married him she'd be Trace Pace.

## MAY 30

Oh golliwobbles, just what I didn't want. Getting a letter is such a major thrill here. You stand there as they call the names out, thinking, 'I won't get one, there'll be nothing for me,' hoping that if you say that enough it'll somehow make you get one. Well, I got one, and now I wish I didn't.

> Dear Lisa,
> I thought I'd write to you to say that I hope we can be better friends. I know you love your Dad and I don't want to come between him and you. But you and Chloe seem to treat me like I'm an enemy, and that's not very comfortable for me. You know, if you took the trouble to get to know me, you might find I'm not so bad! I'm sure we'd be interested in a lot of the same things. I know your Dad was upset at the way you treated me when you were here in the holidays, and I was upset too. So I hope you make a bigger effort next time.
> Yours sincerely,
> Lynette.

Aaaghh, yuk, slime, now what do I do? I don't want to write back. She's already acting like she owns Dad. Right now I wish I could talk to Chloe.

## May 31

Can't write much—I'm drowning in Crusaders and Moslems. At least I've got some good books—Cathy and I are sharing some. Normally Ann gets into the Library before anyone else and corners all the books, but she's still in Japan, ha ha. She'll be so crapped off.

Speaking of people being crapped off, Sophie was up a tree, my tree, having a smoke when the branch snapped and down she went. She twisted her ankle and cut her head. I think it was my tree getting its revenge on Soph for poisoning it with nicotine. Soph didn't think that was too funny when I suggested it—guess it wasn't really. But I didn't know my tree was so popular. I reckon Sophie's accident prone.

We've got the topic for the next debate, on top of everything else. It's 'Life is Bliss'. We're saying it is. But I don't know. I look around me and see Marina huddled in a corner, Cathy writing letters for Amnesty, Soph painting her fingernails with liquid paper and felt pens, Kate asleep at her desk, Emma going through the hymn book singing us verses from her favourite hymns, and Tracey sand-papering her new DB's to try to make them look old. This is bliss?

## June 1

Something very strange is going on with Peter. During the holidays we agreed we'd go to the Mortal Danger Concert in August and I gave him $35 for a ticket. When the tour was cancelled I asked him for my money back and he made some vague excuse. Since then I've asked him twice on the phone. It's starting to bug me—it sounds like he's trying to sleaze out of it.

Alex Bear had a particularly bad night tonight. Soph kidnapped him and hid him and wouldn't tell me where. I turned the dorm and the Prep Room upside down, with Soph going 'You're getting warmer' . . . 'colder' . . . Finally I found him—she'd hung him out the window from a long string— and upside down at that. Poor Alex, he has a hard life. I don't think Sophie's very kind to Teddies. Cathy's got a family of Bears and others, so many she can hardly fit in her own bed. Anne's got a few, Trace has a koala called Ned Good, but all Soph has is a Barbie doll that she's punkified: she dyed her hair, gave her a mohawk, pierced her ears, painted tattoos on her, and put a ring through her nose.

Trace's koala is so lifelike, and so big. Miss Curzon picked it up one day and said 'Goodness Tracey, this koala is so heavy! What's it got in it?' and Trace just answered 'Koala.'

I like that. If koalas are full of koala then I suppose humans are full of human.

I'm feeling guilty about Alex. I forgot to take him for the holidays so the poor thing had to sit sadly on his own in the dorm the whole time. Is this what growing up does to you? You forget your best friends? I know I'll always love Alex, the whole of my life, but maybe adults don't have time for Teddy Bears.

## JUNE 5

This Crusades assignment is going to end with my throwing myself off the top of the clock tower. It's too much. I did hardly anything else all weekend. Ann got back yesterday and went white when she realised what she'd missed. She's started on it already. No doubt she'll be in front of me by the end of the week.

I shouldn't backstab her though. She actually gave me a present from Japan—she had something for everyone in the dorm. Mine was a writing pad of the most beautiful handmade paper.

We played basketball again Saturday morning and lost 14–30. It's a bit of a rip-off—we're the only sport with Saturday matches at the moment. I don't mind that—I enjoy playing—but it makes it harder to find a team. People get so bitchy about it—it's not my fault that we have to play.

I tried out for 'Flowers for Algernon' on Saturday too. That's the school play. It looks like it'll be a good play but I don't know how I went. It's hard being Year 9—you'd never get a big part. But at least nearly everyone in this dorm had a go.

But the main thing this weekend was my big fight with Peter. I rang him Saturday night and somehow we got onto the subject of the Mortal Danger $35 again. It's obvious that he's spent the money and he's trying to put me off till he can get some more from his parents. What a low-life. We ended up having a terrible fight and I hung up on him. I just can't believe he's done this. Guys really are jerks. They're such users. Well, he's used me for the last time. I'd rather talk to his parents than to him. How'd they come to have such a drop-kick for a son?

*JUNE 7*

Chloe rang tonight, in a bad way. It's funny, we've never discussed each other's problems much, but suddenly she rings me like this and talks and talks, and cries too. Things don't sound too good. She reckons Dad'll get married to Lynette, and she can't stand Lynette. The worst thing for Chloe is that she's moved back in with Dad, and it was working quite well, but she says she couldn't live under the same roof as Lynette.

I still don't like Lynette that much either. She's OK I guess but if Dad gets married—well, I don't know, it seems like he's breaking things up even more. First there were the arguments, and the silences, then they moved to different houses, then they got divorced, then they started making new friends, and mixing with new groups of people . . . now, if Dad gets married again, where will it all end? It seems to go on for ever, further and further away from the life we used to have. I feel myself reaching back for it, like someone being washed out to sea, grabbing at the shore, my fingers leaving lines in the sand as the tide drags me away. I want to be back on the beach, on the hot dry beach.

The thing is, despite everything, I still like to think I'm a fighter, that if I work hard enough at something I can change it, that what I achieve is up to me. But with Mum and Dad, I don't seem to have any influence over what happens. They keep doing all these things, one after another, and they never even tell me—I find out about them indirectly or by accident, or when someone bothers to tell me.

I'm glad Chloe rang, though. I only wish I could have found something good to say to her. I couldn't think of anything much.

I'm meant to be preparing for this debate. 'Life is Bliss?' Famines, floods, fires, AIDS. On the other hand chocolate, rowing, guys (sometimes), friends, teddy bears, trees, music . . .

It's Marina's birthday today, so we all partied on, on her behalf. She had a lot of tuck actually—first time ever—and she shared it round at supper.

No-one wanted to take much, because it's so unusual for her to have anything, but we ate some. She would have been hurt if we hadn't.

She got such a shock this morning—we all had presents for her, and we sang 'Happy Birthday' and all that stuff. I honestly don't know if she enjoyed it or not but I'm glad we did it. I gave her a Genetic Defects tape, and a poster of Jerome Vary (although that just comes with the tape). She got some good pressies.

## JUNE 8

I've got so many Crusades books on my desk that there's hardly any room for this Journal. Mr Lindell, if you ever do read this, I'm sorry it's a bit patchy at the moment but all my thoughts seem to be in the twelfth century.

We play Crusaders at basketball on Saturday, and they're the top team, so it must be an omen. Maybe we should dress like the Turks. I don't think it'll help though.

Sophie and I both got in 'Flowers for Algernon', but I've got what must be the smallest part. I say one line: 'Doctor, may I change the bed?' Well, it'll be fun anyway. I'm just glad to be in it. Soph's surprised everyone by scoring quite a good role— she's a girl called Gina, who's a real tumper, rough as guts. Miss Knight-Fox is producing it—I think she likes Soph.

## JUNE 9

Soph's got this stupid new saying, where every time she gets criticised for any little thing she says, 'Oh, sorry, I'll slash my wrists.' She said it this morning when Ann got mad at her for spilling her shampoo; she said it in Maths when she'd forgotten to bring Rikki's calculator; she said it at supper when I realised she'd drunk all the milk. It's so annoying. It's not even funny.

## June 11

Dad and Lynette actually visited today. I'm surprised Dad knew where the school was. The first thing I noticed is how he's trying to look all young again for Lynette. He was wearing these trendy Spike clothes and his new glasses and, I couldn't believe this, he's had the BM sprayed black. I mean, honestly. I was just glad none of my friends were around. I suppose he and Lynette looked all right together in a way, 'cos she does dress well—people notice her. She's quite stunning-looking really—she's got this short haircut and she's tall and she was wearing a great Zodiac silver jacket.

I thought she'd be all sickly nice again, but she wasn't. She was friendly but kept her distance. Maybe she was waiting to see what I'd be like. No-one mentioned the letter—I certainly wasn't going to bring it up. Maybe I'll write her an answer one day.

I showed her round the school, with Dad of course, and she didn't say anything too dumb, except for asking Miss Curzon if she was a prefect. I don't know, maybe Miss Curzon was flattered.

## June 12

Glory be, we're having a Year 9 dance! This is the biggest miracle in 2000 years. Mrs Graham announced it at Roll Call—the words were squeezed out of her like juice out of a peanut. You could tell it wasn't her idea. I've been here a year and a half and this is the first time anything like this has happened. It's four schools—boys from St Patrick's (Emma's happy) and St Luke's, girls from Girls' Grammar and Warrington. At least it's not Walford College, so I won't be seeing good old Pete. But no doubt Huw'll be there. Oh well, I'll survive.

We're even getting a band—Mrs Graham didn't know who, needless to say. Wonder if Genetic Defects are free that night? If it was left to Mrs Graham we'd have the 2nd Mt Sandon Boy Scout Tin-Whistle Orchestra.

Cathy and I did Marina's hair tonight, or as much as she'd let us. It was like trying to touch a wild deer. But we brushed it out and cut it a bit shorter. She wouldn't let us touch the fringe, which I think's too long, but I can understand why she might want it that way. She has got nice hair, though. It's frustrating that she won't let us do much with it.

Soph and Emma have got a craze for aerobics at the moment and every night they do all these exercises. They do them just before lights out and it always ends in a mess: they beg the teacher not to put the lights out till they've finished, and the teacher gets impatient and makes them get into bed, then two minutes later they're out of bed and doing them in the dark, then the teacher comes in and catches them and sends them downstairs. Almost every night that happens. Anyway, they're doing them at the moment during Prep. Emma's doing snapbacks and chanting, 'I must, I must, increase my bust.' Good luck Em. She'll get caught sooner or later.

Oh, Mr Lindell, there is so much I didn't know before this Crusades assignment. Did you know the first Crusade was led by a couple of beggars? (They got wiped out.) Did you know Richard the Lion Heart was a pretty slack King? Did you know Robin Hood mightn't even have existed? Did you know the Christians used pictures of Saracen horses pooing in the Holy Sepulchre to get the other Christians mad?

They all died in the worst ways. King John ate too many peaches and drank too much new cider. Barbarossa drowned because he went swimming straight after a meal. King Richard got shot in the shoulder and died of gangrene after they cut the arrow out. The guy who shot him was flayed alive. That is really utterly absolutely disgusting. It wasn't his fault—he was only doing his job.

I still don't like the Crusades much. I'm sick of them. There's nothing that interesting about them.

JUNE 15

I hate assignments. I hate tests. I hate the Crusades. I hate Prep. I hate History. I hate Science. I hate French. I hate Divinity. I hate Chapel. I hate School food. I hate boarding. I hate all the stupid rules and regulations. I hate Mrs Graham. I hate Dr Thorley. I hate Mr Hardcastle. I hate Matron. I hate the way the school doctor makes you take off all your clothes when you're only there for a sore toe. I hate the kind of music Kate plays at full volume every chance she gets. I hate the way Sophie spits all the time. I hate how fat and disgustingly ugly I am. I hate the way the seniors keep pushing you off the phone. I hate the way even the dogs are kept on chains all the time in this school, and any time a stray comes on campus and all the kids start feeding it and looking after it Matron calls the Pound straight away. I hate it how the Year 11s and 12s never talk to you and treat you like dirt. I hate the way everyone here dresses the same, and anyone who dresses differently is treated like she's infectious. I hate how Ann makes herself vomit so she can get out of basketball practice. I hate myself for being so vague (I took a shower tonight with my headphones still on). I hate the way my parents never take me out on weekends. I hate it how Mum and Dad never tell you what's going on and when you ask they just say 'nothing' or tell you something that's about one-tenth of the real story and sounds harmless. I hate this feeling of endlessly going through the same jumble over and over again, in my mind and my life. I feel like I'll never get anywhere till I sort it all out. I hate what I nearly did just over a year ago. I feel like it's a big dark shadow inside me that I'll never get rid of. I hate wasting so much time writing in this Journal when I could be doing something useful. I hate how slack our basketball team is. I hate how Marina never talks. How can she hope to get anywhere if she won't talk about it? I hate the way I've written all this ugly stuff. I hate how I've sat here all night and got nothing done.

*JUNE 16*

God I really started something tonight. I wrote a whole lot of questions to Marina—one by one—and she kept answering them, so I just kept on going. I hope I did the right thing. She ended up crying and crying like no-one I've ever seen before. She seems OK now. I hope that Mrs Graham doesn't find out. I think I put my foot in it, my whole leg maybe.

## JUNE 20

We had the debate tonight, after two postponements. We don't seem to have improved much—we lost again, to MLC. They had Caroline Barber as their first speaker—the Barbers were our neighbours at 'Connewarre'. It was good to see her. She asked me to come and stay in the August holidays, but I don't know. I don't know if I can stand to see 'Conne' all run down and with someone else owning it.

Anyway, the debate. Cathy went first and talked about the human things—that was our plan—like family and friends. I went second and did the other stuff—like mountains and sunsets and stars. Sarah was third, and she did mainly rebuttal, plus she talked about how even pain was good because you can't experience the bliss until you've had some bad times to compare it to. I thought we did OK, and some of the audience said we were ripped off, but they're probably a bit biased.

## JUNE 21

Roll on mid-term. Dad rang tonight to say he'd pick me up from here on the Tuesday to go straight to the snow. Chloe's getting a lift up with the Kinrosses.

I've been thinking some more about asking Mr Lindell to read this Journal and I don't think I will. There's too much in it that I wouldn't want him to read—too much personal stuff. I'm scared they'd send me to a shrink if they knew everything. I might let Cathy or someone read it instead.

Sometimes I think I ought to go to see the School Counsellor, see if she can sort out my complicated life. I don't even know her name, but she's meant to be good. Marina practically lives there.

Speaking of Marina, I've been watching her the last few days—since Friday night really. She seems OK, kind of strained, but that's nothing new. Everyone's got the flu anyway, except me. I refuse to get it. Marina is going to Cathy's for mid-term—if she doesn't enjoy that she'll be hard to please.

Kate and Soph and Trace have got some outrageous plan to take an illegal this weekend and go skiing. They're mad, but knowing them they'll probably get away with it. They get away with so much. They want to go with Lisa Chen and Susannah Scotland—should be wild.

Apparently it hasn't stopped snowing for about five days. I'd love to go but I suppose I'll be boring and stay here and finish my Crusades assignment.


## JUNE 22

What is going on? Chloe reckons Mum'll get married too, to some bloke I've never heard of. I don't know if Chloe knows what she's talking about or not. It's just hopeless. Everyone's trying to get out of basketball again—there were eight people with notes at training. What a day.


## JUNE 23

Some sloppy smelly heap of meadow mayonnaise has kleptoed nearly all of my Crusades assignment. I can't believe it. I'm too mad to cry. If I find out who did it I'll give them what the guy who killed King Richard got. Why are some people such utter complete skid-marks? All they left was the Bibliography and the Title Page and one map—don't know why they bothered to leave that even. Maybe I should thank them for leaving it. As it is I went so sick in Prep that I think I've scared them all into silence. Marina looked like she was going to dive under her desk.

I went to see Mrs Graham. She was quite good actually, but I know there's not much she can do. She said people take them because they don't like someone, so they want her to bomb out; or they take them so they can copy and improve their own marks. In the first case, she said, you never catch them because they trash the stuff straight away. In the second case, you can catch them if you see something in their assignment that you recognise as yours, like a sentence in an essay, or a drawing—but she said it's pretty rare.

I wonder if there are people around here who hate me enough to take my assignment just to get me into trouble. Emma went off at me the other night—well at a few of us actually—but I don't think she'd do something like that. I don't think anyone in this dorm would. I figure it's someone from another dorm, although it'd be hard for them to get in and out of here without being seen.

The thing is, I spent so many hours on that thing. There's been a kind of Crusades mania round here the last week or so. People have been getting up at five in the morning to do more work, or sneaking back downstairs after lights-out. I've done quite a bit under my doona with a torch, and last night Cathy and I did some in the Drying Room till after midnight.

I just choke up with anger when I think about it.

## JUNE 26

Handed in what I could of the Crusades assignment. I did two essays over the weekend and one of the maps again and some of the pictures, so in the end I still had a lot less than half. I don't know what'll happen about my mark. Apparently two other people got theirs ripped off too. Dr Whiteley came into our Morning Assembly and made a speech about how disgusting it was and how she wants them returned. Maybe they will be, but I doubt it.

At least I've got plenty of witnesses to the work I did.

## JUNE 27

It's a madhouse here again tonight folks. K, S and T have been busted wide open for last weekend's illegal. Every five minutes another message comes for one of them to go see Mrs Graham, while the other two sit here white-faced. They think they'll be expelled, and I guess there is a chance of that. They are crazy. They play with hand grenades all year long and then they're upset when one of them finally goes off. But they're still getting the giggles every few minutes, even now. What a bunch.

Mrs Graham's interrogation technique is to keep calling you in one by one and checking the stories against each other till she finds a contradiction. Then she goes for the throat. She takes notes while you answer, which helps put you off more. Also she bluffs a lot. Last year there was a ginormous powder/deodorant/moisturiser/toothpaste/shampoo fight in the dorm, right at the end of Prep. I missed it by seconds, because I'd been in the library and was still coming back. But Mrs Graham was convinced I'd been in it and she said Miss Curzon had seen me there, which she couldn't have, and when I asked Miss Curzon she said she'd never said that at all. Talk about getting framed.

Apparently the Housemistress before Mrs Graham was even worse—she had a Breathalyser and she used it to test anyone who'd been out on Exeat. It's hard to believe, but Skye Wills swears it's true. I mean, that is sick.


## JUNE 28

K, S and T have been severely gated—I thought they'd have been suspended at least. All that money Kate's father heaped on the school for tennis courts and the library and everything must have paid off. I reckon I would have gone with them if I'd known I'd just get gated.

I rang Chloe tonight—she's got an exam tomorrow so I thought I'd better tell her to go for gold. She sounded OK—I think she's done a bit more work this year. She needed to—Mum and Dad went sick about her results last year.

Sisters have been living in my brain a lot lately. I'm so curious about Miranda. Is she or isn't she? I wonder if Chloe thinks about her, or worse, if she's ever gone looking for her. It'd be funny if we met in the Dobson Road Milk Bar, opposite Mrs Aston's.

But with all this thinking, I've come to a decision. I'm not going to go there any more, to Dobson Road. That's it now. I want to know the truth about Miranda, but I want it straight. In fact I want it from Dad. I want him to tell me, and I'll wait until he does, and if necessary, one day I'll ask him myself. It may not be for a year or two, but I'll wait. I'd rather do that and have it open. Everyone's been too sneaky about it, operating in the shade, in the shadows. Me included.

It's strange to think I could have a little half-sister. I don't know if I'd ever want to meet her. I'm not very good with those really young kids. I think Miranda's going to have to be shoved into the back of my mind for a while.

It was good tonight though. Chloe and I had a good goss. No-one else wanted the phone for once. But Chloe did say that Lynette's practically moved in to Dad's. She's there all the time. She's got a lot of her clothes there, and she's bought some new furniture for the flat. Sounds like now she's spending Dad's money for him, as if enough people weren't doing that already.

## June 29

Mum called in this afternoon. I was at basketball but she found me, and gave me some tuck, and some clothes I needed for the snow. She was on her way to the McCowans—she's staying there for a few days. She said Chloe cruised through her exam this morning.

It's funny, there she was standing at the end of the gym, with all these bags and parcels, looking a bit self-conscious in such a foreign place, but trying to be cool while she told me all the news and explained what was going down, and there was I in my PE gear, sweaty and red-faced and panting a little, hands on my hips, and feet apart, and in the background was the noise of the ball and the pattering feet and the refs' whistles and the players' calls and I had this huge sudden urge to throw my arms around her and give her a hug and tell her I loved her. I didn't of course, because I wouldn't have wanted her to die of shock, but I did have the urge. Anyway I just thanked her for coming and for bringing the things, and I wished her goodbye and I put the stuff on the side benches. I ran back into the game without looking back, and I guess she went off to the McCowans' place at Longwood.

I'm going to wear jeans to this Year 9 Dance. It'll be a big anti-climax, I think. I can't imagine anything Mrs Graham organising being a really wild night. But I might be wrong. I've got a stunning Koori top that I bought with my Christmas money, so I'll wear that. It's got this wonderful design in gold and black. K, S and T have to do a det on Tuesday night while we party on. Soph's such a joke—she's complaining that the det's illegal, because gating was their only punishment and now Mrs Graham's adding more. Tough, Soph—get yourself a good lawyer.

## June 30

I'm so bored and hyper this week—I don't know why. We haven't had much Prep since the Crusades assignment finished. There're Science and Maths tests on Monday but I'm not in the mood to study. I know I can pass OK anyway.

I think I'll write a description of Kate, for something to do. I remember writing one of Sophie a long time ago in this Journal.

To start with, Kate's bad points are that she's big and lazy and she can be as rough as a downtown dunny. She doesn't give a damn about manners, or things like cheating in tests or lying to a teacher. But she's honest in other ways: for a start, she's honest about herself. Her good points are that she's got a heart of gold. She's loyal to her mates, she'd never dob, she's generous with everything she owns. Or maybe it's that she doesn't care about possessions. If she's going out to play tennis she'll take the nearest racquet, whether it's hers or someone else's. If your Walkman's missing, the first person you ask is Kate—she just picks up the nearest one. Her parents own a string of hotels somewhere in country towns. They've got heaps of money, so maybe that's why she doesn't care about possessions.

Because she's so casual and carefree, not many teachers like her, although she gets on well with some—Miss Curzon, and Mr Ross, which is a bit surprising, but I think he likes the way she's always stirring him.

Kate's got a loud voice: she's biologically unable to whisper. She's also got a huge laugh. When she laughs you either join in or leave the room. The only problem with all this volume is that she snores like a dinosaur. They say there's a snorer in every dorm, and Kate sure rattles the windows and brings down the plaster. I'm used to it now, but it took a while.

I don't think Kate could ever live in a city.

Kate knows more jokes than anyone I've ever met but the trouble is none of them are funny. You do get sick of them after a while—in fact they can get on your nerves if you're a bit down.

Well, Kate Mandeville, this has been your life—from my point of view, anyway.


## July 3

Had nothing to do this afternoon so I tried to ring Mum, got no answer; tried to ring Chloe and got Lynette instead. She said Chloe had gone to the movies with a guy called Brendon—I've never heard of him before. I made the big effort and talked to Lynette a bit. She was pleased, I suppose. She's got a promotion in her job—she's running a new department, looking after Japanese customers or something. I didn't know she spoke Japanese.

I wonder what growing up was like for her. She seems so confident and polished. I wonder if she ever got so depressed she felt like pulling the plug. It's hard to imagine, but you never know with people.

## JULY 4

Dear Lisa,

Oh, so much to say, but I don't know where to start! Lisa, there's a lot about you that I didn't understand before. If only you let people like Sarah and Rikki read this Journal! So many people think you're tough—no, not tough, sorry, that sounds terrible—but strong, and a bit hard to approach. They say you never show your feelings or tell anyone your problems and I think they assume that maybe you don't like them much.

This is coming out badly. What I mean is, everyone likes you, obviously—if they took a vote for School Captain in our year you'd win easily—but maybe they're a bit scared of you. The trouble is, they have long memories, and I think they remember how hard you were with Natasha when her parents separated last year. I don't think anyone realised your parents had just broken up—and of course you, being you, didn't tell anyone.

Things have changed since then, obviously—people like you because you're generous and you're always doing things to help people and you never whinge or backstab. But they still find you hard to get to know.

Reading your Journal has been the first time that I've felt I've really started to get to know you. The things about you and your family—I felt privileged to be allowed to read them. The stuff about Kate and Sophie was really funny. I'd forgotten a lot of the things you've put down here—as you noticed

I don't write so much about school, but I loved some of your stories. I'm glad you liked reading my Journal, too—and I'm glad I showed it to you.

Lisa, I hope we'll be much better friends after this. Have a good rage tomorrow night—there's some real dolls at St Luke's. I can't wait. Have a good mid-term too. I'm so nervous about having Marina to stay, but I'm glad she is.

Heaps and stax of love,     Cathy.


## JULY 5

Dear Lisa,

I hope you won't be angry with me for writing in your Journal. I don't think I'd like anybody to write in mine. But I saw the way you were all swapping Journals last night, so I thought maybe you wouldn't mind.

I wish someone had asked me to write in theirs but I can understand why they didn't.

So, I am a gatecrasher in your book. It's a strange feeling, like I'm talking to you, but with a muffled voice. I wonder if I will have the courage to watch your face as you read this.

Lisa, the thing I find hard right now is that everyone is putting so much pressure on me to talk. I feel they watch me like cats in a garden, waiting for me to speak, to perform.

I can't understand how people can use words so casually. They talk without thinking: they open their mouths and the words run out like water from a tap. I used to be like that once. Now I've learnt that words are precious, dangerous things.

Lisa, please talk to me, make me talk, ask me questions, force me to speak.

I can't stand my own silence.

M.

Help! I've just found this, and she's already left. She's gone with Cathy for mid-term. I wish I could run after their taxi now. Oh, I can't wait to see her next week. But God knows what I'll say when I do, or if I'll be able to say anything.


## July 13

How am I ever going to bring this up-to-date? So much has happened I feel like I'll explode before I can get it down. I knew I should have taken it to the snow but I figured I wouldn't have time to write in it. I wouldn't have, either. It was all action up there—the weather was so great for once, and the snow was the best for years.

Anyway, I'd better start with the hot goss from here. First, Marina saw her father over mid-term, while she was staying with the Preshills. And she talked to him, according to Cathy. Words came out of her mouth! She's sly, the old Marina—she must have planned it all in advance. I still don't know a lot about it, because Cathy hasn't had a chance to tell me much, but she said Marina's father's in a prison camp at Tarpaggi, which isn't far from the Preshills' place at Tregonning. So I guess Marina must have gone to the prison at visitors' hours or something. Wonder if it was like in the movies, with glass screens and telephones? Anyway, Cathy said Marina actually told her she'd seen him, when she got back to Tregonning, and she said, 'Thank you for having me' to the Preshills when they were leaving.

That's all Cathy had time to tell me.

Of course, everyone knows, and they're all watching Marina like foxes but pretending not to. Everyone's hoping she'll suddenly rip off a few thousand words at them. As far as I can see, she doesn't look any different.

It's quite exciting, after what she wrote in my Journal. Cathy must have just about swallowed her teeth when Marina hit her with her first sentence. I hope she'll say something to me soon. I don't feel like trying to force her.

Second bit of goss is not so good. Kate got picked up by the cops last Saturday night. It's the first time I've seen her really worried, and believe me, she is packing her daks. She wasn't going to tell anyone about it, but needless to say the whole Year 9 knew by lights out. She was caught in a stolen car with a guy who was expelled from Brentwood last year. Kate says she didn't know it was stolen but she still might be charged.

Originally she was going to the snow, but when she took that illegal before mid-term her parents cracked a bit of an aggro and cancelled the skiing. Probably would have been better if she'd gone; she wouldn't have got into so much trouble.

The other thing is, she reckons she might get expelled from here, but I can't see how she can, for something that happens during the holidays. You'd think that what she does in her spare time is her own business. Still, I suppose that's not always true. I mean if you got arrested for murder or drug-running or something the school'd have to expel you.

My mid-term wasn't as dramatic as these others. It was OK though. The Year 9 dance was a disaster for me—I spent the whole night trying to avoid these complete drop-kicks from St Patrick's, two guys called Duncan and Wayne. God, they were losers. Plus they would have registered about 0.8 on the breathalyser scale. Then, when I tried to crack onto a guy from St Luke's I crashed and burned badly. Turned out he was with Laura Johns, so that was a popular move with Laura, who would have nuked me if she'd had a button handy.

Anyway, I'd forgotten the whole thing by the end of the first day skiing. I love it so much. Even the arriving is fun—getting to the car park with all these happy people piling out of their cars. Then loading the four-wheel drives and cramming into them, clouds of breath coming out, everyone talking excitedly about what it'll be like and what they've forgotten to bring and how hard it'll be to get into the lodges, with all the snow. I like our flat, too. It's old but it's nice. It feels so good to pour into it, turn on the lights, rush to the heater, check that your skis and and boots are still there, fill the flat with noise and warmth and life. It's strange to think of it up there now, lonely and dark and cold again. It's as though it has to have people there for it to be alive—without them, it's dead. Funny, that.

I skied with different people at different times: with Chloe quite a bit, and Dad of course, and Sophie and Trace (Trace was staying with the Smiths), and the Detwarsiti twins and Rhys Leighton. A strange thing happened with Rhys. I mean, I've known him all my life, and I always thought he was a nice guy and so understanding. Chloe was going out with his brother for a long time—well, a long time by her standards—and both of them often had to baby-sit us, so they used to take us with them when they went places.

The last few years I've only really seen Rhys at the snow. Sometimes other places too, but not often. Anyway we were sitting on West Ridge chair, which is the longest ride on the mountain, and Rhys took my hand to look at my heat sensitive watchband that Dad gave me, and the next thing he said was, 'God I like you Lisa.' And I suddenly realised how much I liked him, and always had, and suddenly there we were having a great big wonderful tonguey. It was hard to get off the chair at the end of the ride—we nearly went round for another circuit. Considering that a few weeks ago I'd given up on guys for life, it all happened a bit quickly, but we had the best time. We were just together for every moment from then on. We went to Ronnie's and the Spit and Mogul Munchies. I felt so contented and happy with him. Everyone kept saying how much I'd changed, but I don't know about that.

I nearly told Rhys my biggest darkest most wicked secret. I didn't but maybe I will one day. I feel I can talk to him about anything.

## JULY 14

Gee I let rip in this Journal last night. I wrote most of it under the doona by torchlight. I haven't been game to read it back and probably never will, but at least the handwriting guarantees that no-one else will be able to read it either.

Think I'll burn this thing at the end of the year. It's too dangerous to leave lying around.

Got a det from Mr Lindell today for not concentrating when we were meant to be answering questions about 'Man Friday'. This is definitely Rhys' fault—he should do the detention for me.

Everyone's hanging out for Marina to start chatting away like a pet parrot but not a word so far. Maybe Cathy dreamt the whole thing. I haven't said anything to her yet. I don't know whether I should or whether I should give her more time.

I'm worried about Kate, though. She really is in a bad way. I've never seen her so upset. I suppose it is pretty serious. I'd forgotten she got picked up for shoplifting in Tozers last year too, so that wouldn't impress the cops or Dr Whiteley. She had to see Dr Whiteley today.

Surely it's not a crime to be in a stolen car if

you don't know it's stolen? Guess it depends on what the guy said. Kate's saying now that he's a real drop-kick, but it's a pity she didn't figure that out before last weekend.

I went for a long run today—did the Horseshoe course twice. It felt good! I've been getting too slack.

## JULY 15

Mum's taking me out tomorrow. She's coming to watch us play basketball, then taking me and Cathy to lunch. Funny, a year ago it would have been Issy and Kizzy, no questions asked. Friendships change so much. We just say hello when we pass each other now.

I did ask Sophie, but I forgot she's gated.

I'm glad Mum's coming. I really want to see her, somehow. It'd be good to have time to talk.

Rhys rang before Prep. We talked for about half an hour. We just seem to talk so easily. He told me he's liked me ever since years ago when we were at the Beatty Heads Tennis Tournament. I remember that day. He was so cute.

## JULY 18

Well, it happened this afternoon. The proof that Cathy didn't dream it after all. Marina and I were the only ones in the dorm. I'd come back from a crossie, had a shower and came into the dorm still drying myself. Deciding I needed a sugar charge, I opened my tuck box. It was reasonably full, thanks to Mum's visit on Saturday. I'd already opened a packet of Chocolate Clouds, so I took a couple out to munch on. Then, with the tuck box still open, I said to Marina, 'Hey Marina, you want a biscuit?'

She said, 'Yes please.' I said 'Chocolate Clouds OK?' and she said, 'Yes, thank you.' I suddenly realised that she'd spoken and like an idiot I went, 'Aaaghh! You talked to me!' Then I got the giggles.

Boy, did I feel like an idiot.

Trying to choke down my giggles I gave her a couple of biscuits. Then I said, 'Sorry, but I did get a shock.' She'd had a little smile on her face and then it spread and became a big smile. She was blushing, and she looked really pretty. She said something then that I'll never forget. She said: 'Thank you for being nice to me this year.' I got a bit red, and said, 'Don't be stupid' which wasn't very encouraging to say to someone who hadn't spoken for so long. It'll be my fault now if she never speaks again. I don't think either of us knew what to say next, but a moment later Soph and Trace came bursting in with Rikki Martin, all laughing and yelling, so that was the end of that.

The other thing I wanted to write about tonight was seeing Mum on Saturday. It was good actually. We only went to Pizza Hut for lunch, but after we got back here and Cathy said good-bye to Mum, I just sat in the car and talked. Mum didn't seem in any hurry to go. The only time she got a bit annoyed was when I asked if she and Dad might get together again. I suppose it was a stupid question. She did say she thought it was possible that Dad would marry Lynette. She said she didn't have any plans like that, which was a relief to hear.

I told her about Kate and the cops, and Marina seeing her father and talking to the Preshills, and about Peter ripping me off for $35. I don't know why—I don't normally tell her all that school stuff and boyfriend stuff. I was just in a mood to talk I guess.

She said a strange thing. She said, 'People try so hard to destroy themselves.' I was surprised. Then she added, 'The only cure is to care about as many things as you can.' I thought about that time at Dad's flat. I hadn't cared about anything then, or anyone, including myself. This year was better—I care about Marina and Cathy and Trace, and lately Soph and Kate too (I hardly notice Ann and Emma). I care about my family more. I care about rowing, and doing well in school. I care an awful lot about Rhys. I still think I should widen my horizons—maybe I should join Greenpeace and Amnesty and all those organisations that Cathy's in.

## July 19

We got the Crusades assignments back today. I didn't want to look at mine but eventually I did. There were two marks on it—28% for the work I'd done, and 86% which is what I'd have got if the whole assignment had been done to the standard of the bits that I'd handed in.

Now it's up to Dr Thorley to decide what mark I'll get. It's important—it's worth 40% of the term mark.

I wrote a long letter to Rhys, which hasn't left much time to do this.

## July 20

I went for a run in the rain this afternoon. It was wonderful—it was raining fairly hard when I started but after a few minutes it eased off into a steady but gentle drizzle. Just little light drops falling softly on you. In the distance you could see the sky starting to clear, and some watery looking sunshine. My run became more like a dance than a run. I was doing pirouettes and all kinds of funny movements. No tumpers following or watching, thank goodness.

It's against the rules to run on your own now, but I do it all the time, with no great dramas.

Tonight, in this Prep, we just had the best moment of the year. Emma asked if anyone could lend her a calculator but no-one could, or no-one wanted to. Then just as she'd given up, Marina suddenly said, in a quiet little voice: 'You can borrow mine if you want, Emma.' It's the first time she's said anything in a group, as far as I know. It's certainly the first time she's said anything to this dorm. Then quick as a flash Sophie said, in her fake school-teacher voice: 'Marina, I wish you'd stop talking in Prep.' Everyone just cracked up. Even Marina smiled a bit.

This is a pretty good dorm I think. I didn't like it at the start of the year but I like it now. Last year we got changed around at the end of Second Term. I hope that doesn't happen again this year.


JULY 25

Poor Kate is going to be charged by the cops. She found out a few minutes ago—her parents rang up. She's on her bed now—she's absolutely bawling. Sophie's in there with her. I don't think the school's going to expel her or anything. They wouldn't want to. I'd go straight to Dr Whiteley if they tried, and so would a lot of other people.

It's hard to find out the facts, though, because Kate—I don't mean this in a nasty way—does make everything so dramatic. It sounds, from what she reckons her parents said, that she'll most likely get put on a good-behaviour bond, which isn't great, but it's definitely better than some of the other possibilities. Apparently the solicitor is telling her to plead guilty. One thing that Kate said tonight, when she was crying, was strange, though. She said, 'I told him he'd get caught.' That makes it sound like she did know the car was stolen.

I don't blame her if she lied to us about it. I guess anyone would.

I wish I wouldn't keep noticing things like that. I'm sure nobody else does. It makes relationships so complicated.


## JULY 26

Bonus! Here's the first of many (I hope) letters from Rhys.

Dear Lisa,

How are you, Lise? Is your life overflowing with bubbles at the moment? I'm pretty up. Paul Lim is here and he sends his love. Not his lust, just his love. I send both. By the way, are you free on the 27th for a party at the Kenners'? Just watch out for me in the holidays—I'm armed, legged and dangerous.

I've had a good day. Jacob and I finally got permission to start a Book Club. It'll be cool in the school. We're going to have meetings, with book reviews and readings and discussions about the right of Stephen King to exist in a school library. I think he has every right; Jacob doesn't, neither does our librarian.

Tomorrow we've got an excursion to see a play for English, so there's no Homework tonight. That's why I'm free to write to you. This afternoon we beat Michener 2–0 and guess who scored both goals? YES! That's right! Not me. It was John Kazlowski. Guess who scored nothing? YES! Right again.

OK Lise, gotta go. Be well, remember I love you deeply. Seriously. Lots of that stuff,

Rhys

Dad called in again yesterday, with Lynette. The best thing about mid-term was that Lynette doesn't like skiing, so she didn't come. Hope she never gets a taste for it. I think I'm safe though—Paradise for Lynette is Hudson Island, lying in the sun having some guy in a white coat bring her drinks on a silver tray.

## July 27

Sophie and I have been terrorising Year 8. This morning we were coming out of the Library when we heard two Year 8 kids calling Marina 'pizza face'. She just kept walking and so did we, but when Marina was out of sight we went looking for them. We found them. I was all fired up and I opened my mouth to let them have it, but before a word came out this volcano erupted beside me. It was Soph. She was amazing. She scared me even. If you put an H-bomb inside a volcano—well, that's roughly what it was like. She just engulfed those kids with abuse. She didn't spill any blood but I think they got the impression that if they ever tried to pay Marina out again they would be shredded and dried and used for fish food. In the end I didn't have to say a word—I just went quietly away with Soph when she was finished.

Had to interrupt this for a phone call. It was Chloe—she's got her licence at last. I don't believe it. This was her third attempt. She's a good driver but she kept failing on technicalities. She wants to drive down to see me next weekend. It's Parents' Day, with all the displays and games and stuff. Dad said that he'd be here for it. I might ring him after Prep and remind him.

I'm still thinking about today's English—we had to write a list of things we believed in, and say why we believed them. It was so hard, much harder than I thought it'd be. I know I still believe in God, even though I don't like Chapel services much. But there has to be a God, doesn't there? I mean, take the pen I'm writing this with. If you unscrew all the bits, there's five separate parts. Now, I can put it back together, using my brain and eyes and hands. But if I just leave the pieces lying on my desk they'll stay there forever, five separate bits. If that's true for something simple like a pen, how did something as complicated as this planet get put together? I think there had to be a God to do it.

I believe in the power of friendship. I believe in music. I believe that people who are terminally ill shouldn't be kept alive by machines, unless they want to be. Um, what else? I believe we've badly damaged this planet—maybe past the point of no return.

I believe people have to take charge of their own lives and try to get themselves through the things that happen to them, instead of rushing to the authorities for help when they have problems.

That's all I can think of, and it's a lot more than I wrote in class!


*JULY 28*

We started Sex Ed today, with a lady who comes to the school especially to teach it. We have it one period a week till the end of next term. She sure didn't hold back. I don't know whether I wanted that amount of detail. The best moment was when she launched into a graphic description of the things guys do when they're coming on hot and heavy, and Emma let out this long low groan of disgust. She didn't mean anyone to hear, but we all did. The whole place cracked up.

We haven't got much Prep tonight, so I've just been sitting here day-dreaming. To be honest I've been thinking about Rhys and when we were dancing at Mogul Munchies. The way his hands kept touching me, and that little bit of extra pressure sometimes, just when you don't want it and where you don't want it. OK, I know I'm lying—I wanted it. Anyway, suddenly Sophie said to me: 'What are you smiling about Lisa?' It was quite embarrassing. I couldn't think of anything to say, just sat there blushing.

I'd better get my mind onto something ordinary, before I really give myself away. Today seemed to be devoted to doing stuff for Parents' Day—getting ready, I mean. Instead of History, for instance, we got conscripted to move chairs to the Dining Room for the Orchestral Concert. Then we spent Maths helping put up displays in the Library. There's a few poems I wrote that are being used in an English display and a kind of wreath thing that I made in Ceramics is in a glass case in the foyer, so I've scored a few honourable mentions.

Dad said he's definitely coming but he'll be a bit late. He said he'd bring Lynette. I tried to sound enthusiastic.

I wonder if Marina's mother will come again. I'd love to have a good long conversation with Marina, and find out heaps and heaps about her, but it's not going to happen for a while. She does say things now but only one sentence at a time, and only factual sort of things. She asked me where our Maths class had gone today, when I ran into her near the classroom. And she'll ask you to pass the bread at meals. That's all, but it's a lot better than it was. It must be so hard for her. I wonder if she'll go and see her father again these holidays. Cathy said she didn't go to the prison—she found out her dad went to Buntleigh Hospital once a week, so she met him there. It's strange that she wanted to—I would have thought that she'd be happy never to see him again, after what he did to her.

I wonder if she writes to him. She sits at her desk like a little hamster—I don't know what she's thinking, or doing. She writes heaps in her Journal, and has done since the start of the year, but God knows what's she's writing about. One time when she was in Sick Bay Sophie wanted to read it, but Cathy and I wouldn't let her.

Sometimes I think Marina and I have a lot in common, but if I ever said that to anyone they'd just laugh.

## August 2

Only two weeks to go till the holidays. I'd do anything to speed it up—compress the two weeks to two hours. I'm so sick of this place. It's the petty rules, the little niggling things that get to you. Your life's not your own, you're constantly getting picked at: 'Hurry up, don't be late.' 'Don't use that door.' 'You've failed Inspection again.' 'Matron wants to know why you didn't get your medication.' 'You've had Bank already this week—you'll have to wait.' 'Clean your locker.' 'Stop talking.' 'Where have you been?'

And when you're on your own for any time at all—like, up your tree—everyone comes after you. 'Are you all right?' 'Are you OK?' 'What's wrong?'

You feel like you're suffocating.

Dad rang tonight. He didn't even turn up on Parents' Day and when I asked him, he just said, 'Oh yeah, sorry, I had to go into work,' as though he hadn't even remembered he was meant to be here.

I'm staying with him for the first week of the holidays again. Chloe'll still be there anyway, and I'll have heaps of time to see Rhys.

## August 3

Kate had to go off with her parents today, to see a solicitor and the Police. She didn't say much about it when she got back—just that she had to make a statement and the case won't be heard for a few months. They've all told her she'll get put on a bond.

She's kind of calmer about it these days, but she's changed—she's a lot quieter. You don't notice her around the dorm nearly as much.

I had tea with Marina tonight. It was good. We chatted away like old buddies. Well, that's a slight exaggeration. Marina said about twenty words, but they were all good ones. I was talking about Kate, and Marina suddenly said: 'Kate lives her life on the outside.' I nearly choked on my baked potato. That's the most intelligent thing I've ever heard anyone in Year 9 say. I know what she meant. With Kate, everything's public, you see and hear everything that happens in her life. With Marina it's all private, all happening inside. Same as me.

Everyone seems to be surprising me with wise comments lately, like Mum the other day. They're all so smart. Makes me feel about as smart as an ironing board.

Marina's voice is soft but every word is clear. It's like everything goes still when she talks. You find yourself sitting there with your fork halfway to your mouth, waiting for her to finish what she's saying.

I don't even notice the burn marks on her face any more.

We've got one more debate this term. I've done all the organising again but I'm not in the team. Cait Henry's taken my place. I'm going to chair it, though. The topic is 'Schooldays are the happiest days of your life.' We're the Opposition. That should be easy!

Marisa just gave me a Prefects' Det for not putting the laundry bags out. Honestly, doesn't that prove what I wrote last night? I mean, I know it's my job, but it's the first time I've missed this year, and I did them in the end. I am extremely cut, in fact I'm chainsawed.

As I was coming out of the year 12 studies I heard Sibella Abbott say to another girl, 'When you're doing inverse functions, does the range of g become the domain of f?' I rushed back here and wrote it down. She might as well have been speaking another language. I figure that if I ever learn enough to be able to understand that sentence, I'll have made it. But it's hard to imagine that in three short years I could be talking like that.


## August 4

Another day drags by, another day closer to the holidays. One class after another, sitting in straight rows while a teacher sits (or stands) out the front and talks at us. Do they really think we're listening, or taking it in? Have I got news for them! Maybe I don't have very good concentration but I tune in for about 5% of it.

English has the most variety but I think Mr Lindell must be tired because it's been fairly dull lately. We're doing a lot of stuff on writing skills.

They should have had a display on Parents' Day of how people really occupy their time during classes. Decorating Homework Diaries, decorating rulers and pencil cases, doodling and sketching, writing on people's arms and legs, tasting every item in a pencil case (Soph did that in Divinity today—she said the liquid paper was the worst), writing notes, seeing how long a strip you can tear a piece of A4 into, seeing how long you can spin a book on top of a ruler, sucking your thumb, counting the number of dots in the ceiling tiles, working out anagrams of your name, trying new signatures . . . You get pretty good at filling in fifty minutes.


## August 6

Well, life just bubbles with surprises sometimes. I've had more visitors this year than I had the whole of last year. Today it was Lynette, on her own. I saw her half-way through our basketball match, standing on the sidelines. I ignored her for a while, partly because I had to concentrate on the game, but then the ball went out of bounds right next to her, and I had to get it, so I said 'Hi' then. But not very friendly. I was confused by her being there.

We lost the game 34–19. If we'd won and Barwon had lost their match we'd have got into the semis, but we lost and Barwon won, so that didn't quite work out. It's good in one way, because the Grand Final's in our holidays so I don't know what we'd have done about that. And at least it means that next week I'll have my first free Saturday for this year.

Anyway, after the game Dr Thorley gave us the usual pep talk, which never works too well because she's so quiet that if you're not a lip-reader you don't pick up a lot. Then I drifted over to Lynette, pretty slow and casual, being rude again. I hate the way I treat her. I hate myself when I'm being like that. But I agreed to have a coffee with her. I didn't have much choice. She said she was on her way to Kennon to see her parents. She said she'd been born in Kennon, which surprised me—she didn't seem like a country girl. And a dairy farm, too. She told me how she and her brother had to hand-milk some of the cows and they used the udders as milk pistols, zapping each other with sprays of milk.

She was OK, nice enough. I'd probably quite like her if she didn't have anything to do with Dad.

Then she asked what I'd thought of her letter. That was awful. I just stared into my coffee, doing a Marina. Finally I said, 'It was OK, I guess.' She said, 'You didn't answer it.' I didn't say anything. Then she said, 'Well, no-one can say I didn't try' and got up and paid the bill and went. That shocked me really—I hadn't expected her to be so annoyed about it. I was pleased in one way, because I don't want to be friendly with her, and I want her to hate me. I want to hate her too. But the way she does things makes me feel so guilty. Maybe she learnt that in her public-relations course.

### AUGUST 8

God, there was the most awful fight tonight. It started with Sophie and Emma, but everyone got involved. I think it was because last night, after lights out, Sophie was having a good old backstab of Marnie Tull, and today Emma told Marnie. Soph started screaming at Emma as soon as she walked in after tea and she didn't stop for the Prep bell or anything else. Some people took Emma's side, some took Soph's. Cathy said Sophie should think before she speaks; Tracey said Emma was two-faced because she's always backstabbing people; Emma said Sophie's two-faced because she's always repeating things other people tell her. I said that anything said in the dorm should be kept in the dorm, and everyone agreed with that, but I don't suppose it'll happen.

So, not a lot of work's been done. It's settled down a bit now. I've been watching Marina—she always looks so frightened when there are fights.

I was going to write to Lynette, but it's too hard to concentrate with everyone yelling at each other. I've written to Rhys instead—it relaxes me to write to him.

Dear Rhys, light of my fridge, it was good to hear from you. It was a choice between writing to you, writing to a witch called Lynette, or doing my Science Prep. It was a hard choice, but you won by a bow-ball.

Tonight's been terrible, one of those nights when you wish you were home, lying on your bed eating chocolate and listening to music. Do you know Sophie Smith? I think you do. She says she knows you, from a party at the Cohens' last year. Anyway, she's in this dorm. Is she ever in this dorm. She's in this dorm like a bomb in a basement. She's spent the last hour going off at a girl called Emma, who I don't think you'd know, because she's from Hong Kong. It's been, like, heavy metal without the music. One thing about Sophie, she lets you know how she's feeling. She doesn't hold back. Bit different from me.

This weekend was incredibly average too. Boy do I sound like a grouch in this letter. We got thrashed in our basketball, smeared from one end of the court to the other. Very messy. So we're out of the comp now—we had to win Saturday.

Thanks for the invitation to the party. Do you really mean it? I'd love to come but it depends who I'm staying with. If it's Dad there's no problem. If it's Mum she wants to know everything, like 'Who are you going with? How are you getting there? What adults'll be there? What time does it finish?' You know how it goes. But I'll try, OK? And I'll let you know.

Time for beddy-byes here. I'd better go. See you—soon I hope. I love you more than chocolate.

Lisa

I sent it like that, except I crossed out the last sentence of the second paragraph, 'Bit different from me', which just proves the point I guess.

## AUGUST 9

Everyone's so tired and bitchy at the moment. It's terrible. We just had another big argument, because I like the window beside me open during Prep and Ann wants it closed. She says it's too cold but I like some fresh air and it gets so hot and fuggy with all the windows shut. I know it's a cold night but I didn't have it open very far. I told Ann she could go do her Prep in the Drying Cupboard— that's the only place where she'd be happy.

Miss Curzon just won a lot of hearts by coming round with a peppermint slice she'd made. Everybody's out of tuck at the moment.

I wrote a short note to Lynette: 'Dear Lynette, I'm sorry if I was rude on Saturday. Thanks for the coffee. Lisa.' I don't know where that leaves us— probably the same place we were at before.

## AUGUST 10

I dreamt about 'Connewarre' last night. I was walking up the hill on the other side of the road, where it's quite scrubby and uncleared. I think I was looking for sheep that might have been missed when we were mustering the paddock, and for some reason Marina was with me. It was cool and shady at the top of the hill and there were no sheep around, so we sat there and talked for a while. But when we were coming down again there were lots of dead sheep everywhere, that we hadn't seen before—piles of old wool and white bones. It was strange.

I think I have to try to realise that I've lost 'Conne'. I torture myself by remembering things about it, but not as often as I used to, I guess. One of the things that made it so good was that I was useful there. I did things that helped the place run better, even things that no-one else realised or knew about, like fixing fences, and putting plumbers' tape on all the pumps and pipes, to stop leaks. I did other things too that somehow made me proud— especially building little shelters for the pumps, out of posts and galvanised iron; and building a new chook house. There's a special feeling about building something—every time you go past it, for ages afterwards, you look at it with a nice glow. Then you come here and you're not trusted to change a light globe.

I took too much for granted there of course. Since I was eight or nine, if I had a job that was a fair distance from the house I'd take a motor bike or a vehicle to do it. It wasn't till a year or so later when there were some American friends of Mum's staying that I realised from the looks on their kids' faces that there was anything special about that. Now I haven't driven a car for a year and a half, and I miss it. There's no feeling quite like it.

Somehow, because of the dream I think, I wanted to ring Dad tonight, so I snuck out of Prep seconds before break, grabbed the phone and was dialling the number as the bell rang. It's the only way you can get a phone round here—three minutes later

there were kids saying 'Are you going to be long?'
Dad was OK. I was scared he'd be angry because
of Lynette but maybe she hadn't said anything,
because he was actually in good form, cracking a
lot of jokes. He said he had a surprise for us in the
holidays—that could be anything from short-
sheeted beds to a week at Disneyland. I asked about
skiing and he said 'Maybe for a couple of days.'

## August 12

We're getting sent to bed for a compulsory early
night. They say it's because we're overtired; I always
think it's because the teachers are feeling slack. It
must be a shocking life for them—having to teach
us all day, then put up with us all night. Still, only
four days to go, and two of those are weekend.

I am going shopping tomorrow with Cathy and
Marina. I know I don't have any money and I'm
pretty sure Marina doesn't, so I hope Cathy's shouting. We'll find something to do, though. It'll just
be good to get out for a while.

Cathy and I don't have any sport, and Marina
never seems to have any—I don't know how she
gets out of it, but she does. I think she gets away
with quite a lot actually.

Rhys has gone on an Athletics camp for the
weekend, so I can't ring him. He's a long-distance
runner. I like that. I'm sick of sprinters.

## August 14

I got really depressed and awful last night, and
desperate thoughts came back into my stupid head
and are still there. I thought it was safe to go anywhere and think anything. Maybe I'll be haunted

all my life. God, if you're up there, keep me safe and alive. Grandma and Grandpa, Nan and Gramps, put in a good word for me.

I had a conversation with Marina tonight that I want to write down so I can remember it. It was after tea and I wandered over to the tree out the front that I used to like to sit in. I haven't been up it for a while. Today was so warm, for winter, and it was still warm after tea, and I felt like being on my own, seeing it's the last night of term.

When I got there, though, I realised I wasn't on my own. Marina was sitting on a stump at the foot of the tree, almost out of sight. But I've seen her there a few times now. So I sat on a rock a bit further around the trunk. 'I'll go if you want,'I said. 'Just say the word.'

'No,' she said. 'We've shared this tree before.'

I nodded.

Then she said: 'I'm saying good-bye to the tree, just in case.'

'What do you mean?' I asked.

'I might be leaving Warrington.'

'What? Why? I thought you liked it here.'

She took a long time between each thing she said, as though she were making sure it'd come out right. Finally she said:

'I like most of it, and I'm glad I came. I'd rather stay here. But my mother doesn't like it. And it is expensive.'

I said: 'You've changed a lot since you've been here.'

She answered: 'I don't know if I have. I've started talking, that's all.'

'You made contact with your father again.'

'Yes, I had to.'

'Why?'

'If I live my life hating him, then I don't have a life.'

'Don't you hate him? I hate him and I've never met him.'

'No. If I hate him it's with all of me. And I don't want to be like that.'

I said: 'But you can't just decide you're not going to hate any more.'

'No. But I found the more I understood him, the less I hated him. And I realised that he's so like me. If I hate him I have to hate myself.'

I said: 'You're different from anyone I've ever met.'

She said: 'I've had more time to think than most people.'


## August 16

Holidays at last. I thought they'd never start.

I decided to bring this Journal with me but I won't be writing in it much tonight. I'm at Dad's; Chloe's here too, and we're going out in a minute with Dad and Lynette, to Giverny, a new French restaurant.

Dad still says he's got a surprise for us tomorrow, but he won't tell us what it is. I suppose that's logical—it wouldn't be a surprise otherwise.

Lynette, I can't make her out. She seems like she's nervous of me now, like kids at school. I don't want that. I never wanted that. It's OK when other people are around, but if we find ourselves on our own in the kitchen or somewhere, she gets a bit embarrassed and awkward. It's awful. I suppose I should have written more in my letter, but I just don't know what I wanted to say.

108

I can't believe this day, any of it or all of it. Now at last I feel I understand Marina a little. Dad went out early. He came back at about twelve o'clock and found Chloe and me and told us to go upstairs and put on our very best clothes. He was dressed up himself, and he was being all funny and excited and mysterious. We couldn't get anything out of him, so we did what he said. Chloe was getting annoyed, and so was I. It took me about twenty minutes, I suppose, but finally I could hear him calling impatiently so I hurried and went downstairs. And I couldn't understand what I was seeing. I stood there thinking, 'I'll make sense of this eventually.' Dad was there, and Lynette—who was dressed like something out of a shop window—and Chloe looking like she was crying and a man in a sports coat and bow tie, carrying a bunch of flowers. Dad said, 'We nearly started without you' then he laughed and said, 'Only joking. As if we would. Come here.' I walked over, with my brain completely out of gear with my legs. He said: 'Now, this is the surprise I promised you. You and Chloe are brides-maids, so big smiles now.'

I don't know if I smiled or not. But I didn't cry. I never do and I never will. The whole thing only took about ten minutes. The man with the bow tie was some kind of marriage celebrant, so he did it all, and Dad and Lynette said sterile things to each other like, 'Our love is as strong as the mountains, as wide as the sky, as old as time.' That's about the only sentence I really heard and it nearly made me vomit. I didn't dare look at Chloe but I think she'd stopped crying. I just looked at the floor.

Then we drank champagne, the bloke with the bow tie went, and Dad took us to The Almond Tree for lunch. Then he gave Chloe heaps of money for us to go out to dinner and do anything we wanted afterwards, and he and Lynette went off to the Hotel Winchester for the night, for their honeymoon.

But Chloe and I, the original party animals, didn't feel like going anywhere. We just came back here and watched TV for a bit. Then, on impulse, I rang Rhys. And to my surprise he came over straight away. It was good to see him. We went up to my room and as soon as I closed the door he said, 'What's wrong?' So I told him. It was funny, I didn't tell him about Dad and Lynette, like I thought I would. Instead I found myself telling him about the terrible time in my room here, that night over a year ago. It seems strange, thinking about it now, as if the pain has gone and it's just a story—even though it's still uncomfortable to remember it. I didn't go into all the gruesome details, how night after night I'd been there on my own, because Dad was always out and Chloe was staying with the Barbers. It was the first holidays since Mum and Dad had separated and I missed 'Connewarre' so badly. Finally, without really thinking about it, I swallowed Dad's tranquillisers. I'd just had enough. I didn't want to fight any more. I couldn't think of anything to live for, and there didn't seem to be any hope of things improving, so I took them.

I read somewhere how when people jump off the tops of buildings or bridges to kill themselves, the ones who survive say that as soon as they jump they start wishing they hadn't, thinking that they've given up too easily. I think now that I'm glad I survived. But I didn't think that then.

Anyway—I did tell Rhys this bit—the big joke was that no-one ever knew what I'd done. I slept for about 24 hours, woke up feeling the worst I've ever felt, and no-one even noticed. It took me ages to work out what day it was—that was bad, switching the TV from channel to channel, trying

110

to match the shows with the TV guide. I guess Dad must have come home late, gone to bed, gone out early in the morning, came home again the next day, and by then I'd been up for a few hours. I even had dinner ready for him. Can't remember what I cooked but I'm sure it was nice.

Later on, before I went to stay at Mum's, I put some vitamin tablets in his tranquilliser bottle. I hope they gave him some good nights' sleep.

Rhys was pretty shocked I think. I don't blame him for that—I've been in permanent shock for a year about it. But he was good. He said I have to stop being so strong and admit that there are times when I need help. He made me promise to ring him if I ever feel like offing myself again. He said he sees the counsellor at his school sometimes, when things get too much, 'cos of course his family's pretty stuffed.

Doesn't he realise I'm Superwoman?

Nice guy though.

We talked for hours. He went about one thirty, then I started writing this. It's three o'clock now and I don't seem able to stop. It's funny, I haven't read this Journal back since I started, apart from the occasional browse. But I remember how at the start I thought it was such an annoying idea. Especially when I realised Mr L wasn't going to be reading them—I couldn't see the point, even though I realised later some people had arranged for him to read theirs. I've changed my mind quite a bit since then, I admit. I suppose it's the way schools make you, that you don't know whether your work is worth anything until a teacher tells you it's OK or not. Especially with things you write. So different to life on 'Conne' where you noticed something that needed doing and you did it and you knew by the end whether you'd done a poor job, a good job or a great job.

But, overall I'm glad I kept this Journal. I just counted and found that I've written in it about 120 times. That's quite a lot. It's helped me, I think. I understand myself better now, and I understand Mum and Dad and Chloe and Marina and Cathy and Kate and Sophie better. I'm slowly getting used to the idea that I've lost 'Connewarre' and that Mum and Dad have split up for good (Dad certainly proved that today). Writing about those things has been good for me.

There are two things I've found very hard to think about, let alone write about though. One's the magazine article about Mrs Aston and Miranda that I showed Mum—seems like years ago now. Boy that was a dumb thing to do. 'Gee Mum, how come Mrs Aston doesn't come and stay any more? Doesn't her daughter look like Chloe? Isn't that funny?'

Yeah, real funny Lisa.

The other thing's those tablets. It scares me to think I could have done that.

When I'm older I'd like to have some kind of job with people who feel like they're stuck on a roundabout, no hope of things working out. Be a counsellor or something. Help them to realise that those sick awful feelings might end—'cos you think they'll go on forever, even though they don't.

Well, now, somehow, I've got to get used to the idea of Dad being married to Lynette. Maybe I will, maybe I won't. I think it's more than their being married, though. It's getting used to Dad being so irresponsible and immature. I hate using those words about him, but they're true. It's not all that long since he was my biggest hero. He could do no wrong. I've learnt a lot the last couple of years. Guess it's called growing up.

I wish I could believe that Lynette'll help Dad grow up.

It's four o'clock. Chloe must have gone to bed

hours ago—it's all quiet down her end. I might ask her to come with me to the movies or something tomorrow. We need to be friends, not just sisters. Today proved that.

> *What's become of poor old Lisa*
> *Why's she sitting up a tree sir?*
> *Won't she wave to you or me sir?*
> *Can she see what we can't see sir?*

Maybe I should wave a bit more often. 'No man is an island.' We did that in English. No woman either.

Oh well, time to catch some Z's. Goodnight Ms Journal, my good friend.

John Marsden
## Letters from the Inside

*Dear Tracey*
*I don't know why I'm answering your ad, to be honest. It's not like I'm into pen pals, but it's a boring Sunday here, wet, everyone's out, and I thought it'd be something different . . .*

*Dear Mandy*
*Thanks for writing. You write so well, much better than me. I put the ad in for a joke, like a dare, and yours was the only good answer . . .*

Two teenage girls. An innocent beginning to friendship. Two complete strangers who get to know each other a little better each time a letter is written and answered.

Mandy has a dog with no name, an older sister, a creepy brother, and some boy problems. Tracey has a horse, two dogs and a cat, an older sister and brother, and a great boyfriend. They both have hopes and fears . . . and secrets.

As Mandy and Tracey swap confidences and share the ups and downs of school, home and friends, they get to know every detail of each other's lives.

Or do they?

A powerful, compelling novel which was shortlisted for the 1992 Children's Book Council Book of the Year Award.

John Marsden
## The Journey

By the author of *So Much To Tell You*, *The Journey* is a story of young people in a world so different and yet so like our own. It is a world in which young people must undertake a journey of discovery on their way to becoming adults.

Argus sets out on his journey away from his valley and his parents, never knowing what adventure will befall him next. He learns how to survive in the wild until he meets up with a travelling fair which he joins, becoming the friend of Mayon the storyteller, of Lavolta and Parara—twins who share the same body—and many others.

But it is with the sweet and wise Temora that he learns some of the deepest secrets.

All journeys must find an end. Argus leaves the fair and travels on alone, until his last and greatest adventure beckons him home. There he tells, for the approval of his elders, the seven stories which are now his story. But all is not done.

There is one more chapter to be lived out in the story of Argus.

'. . . an extraordinary book . . . I would commend it to everybody. Although ostensibly it's a children's book it's something that any adult can read with great pleasure. It's one of those books that don't actually belong to any particular age group . . . like *The Snow Goose*.' TERRY LANE, ABC RADIO

John Marsden
**Out of Time**

James reads by his open bedroom window at night. Other lives and other worlds beckon. One of these worlds is conjured by old Mr Woodforde, a physicist who looks more like an accountant and who constructs a strange black box.

One day when James slips into the laboratory, he makes a dreadful discovery and learns to master a great power.

Who is the little boy in Mexico who scratches pictures of aeroplanes in the dust? How will the girl caught in a wartime bomb blast be reunited with her parents? And why does James sit alone in his island of silence?

With *Out of Time* John Marsden has produced a novel that will further enhance his reputation as one of the most successful writers of fiction for teenagers. This is a challenging novel which poses a new question on every page as it draws us into an ever-widening series of mysteries, into magical, dangerous worlds—in and out of time.